A German Soldier in South West Africa

A German Soldier in South West Africa

Recollections of the Herero Campaign 1903-1904

Peter Moor's Journey to South West Africa

Gustav Frenssen

Translated by Margaret May Ward

With a Short Account of the German South West Africa Campaign by Francis J. Reynolds

LEONAUR

A German Soldier in South West Africa
Recollections of the Herero Campaign 1903-1904
Peter Moor's Journey to South West Africa
by Gustav Frenssen
Translated by Margaret May Ward
With a Short Account of the German South West Africa Campaign
by Francis J. Reynolds

FIRST EDITION

Leonaur is an imprint of Oakpast Ltd

Copyright in this form © 2017 Oakpast Ltd

ISBN: 978-1-78282-680-4 (hardcover)
ISBN: 978-1-78282-681-1 (softcover)

http://www.leonaur.com

Publisher's Notes

Contents

This book is dedicated with tender and loving memories to the cause which the translator hoped it might aid, the cause for which she was always ready to give her abounding strength, and to the service of which she brought the wisdom of a loyal nature and a noble mind,—to the cause of peace.

A. H. W.

Translator's Preface

I have always felt that all war stories dwell too much on the glory and glamour of war, and too little on the hardships and horrors and the unnecessary cruelty of it; and so, when I read a little German book about the South West African war of 1903-04, I wished that everyone else might read it. To me it was absorbingly interesting and beautifully told. This summer I have translated it in the hope that it will affect other people as it affected me.

Margaret May Ward. Temple, New Hampshire, 1907.

CHAPTER 1

Peter Enlists

When I was a little boy I wanted to be a coachman or a letter-carrier; that pleased my mother very much. When I was a big boy I wanted to go to America; then she scolded me. So, when my schooldays were at an end I said one day that I should like best to be a sailor; then she began to cry. My three little sisters wept, too.

But on the day after I left school, before I knew really what was happening to me, I was standing at the anvil in my father's shop, and our apprentice, who had strayed out of Saxony to us and had already worked a long time with my father, was saying to me: "See! there you stand, and there you will stand till you are grey"; and he laughed. As we had a good piece of work, making a gate and paling in front of a fine new building on Broad Street, I was contented, and remained three years in my father's workshop and worked with him and the apprentice, and went evenings to the trade-school. Twice I took a first prize.

In the second year of my apprenticeship, when I was seventeen years old, I met Henry Gehlsen on the street. I sometimes used to play with him as a boy. He was the son of Gehlsen the teacher, who had formerly held a position in our school and was now a principal at Hamburg. Henry was some years older than I and was a student at Kiel. While we were walking together down Breitenburg Street, he told me that he wanted to enlist in the autumn of 1903 for a year in a naval battalion. I asked him why he wanted to enlist in that especially. He replied: "It is fine company. And then, too, it is possible that one can travel at the expense of the government, for if an insurrection breaks out in any of our colonies, or if anything is the matter in the whole world, the naval force is the first of all to be called out."

I did not say anything further on the subject; but I thought to

11

myself that I also might later go into the marine corps. I had already been several times at Kiel and I liked the uniform. What he said about traveling across the seas pleased me too. But at that time, I didn't know how I was going to bring it all about.

One day, in the following year, I learned from an older schoolmate who was serving at Kiel in the 85th regiment, that the navy was enlisting volunteers for three years. That same evening, while I was clearing up and my father was passing through the shop with his short pipe in his mouth, to look out on the street a little, as he always did of an evening, I asked him if I should apply. That pleased him, for he had served with the 31st in Altona till he had reached the rank of non-commissioned officer. He said nothing more than, "Your mother will be frightened at the word 'sea.'"

"Yes," I said; "she has the three girls, though."

"Go and put your case before her," he said; "she is in the kitchen."

Meanwhile she had come out of the kitchen into the shop, and she said, as if she mistrusted something: "What are you two putting your heads together about?" She suspected something because it was the night before a holiday and the work was done.

My father replied: "The boy wants to volunteer for the naval corps in Kiel. You mustn't be afraid. It's called the sea-battalion because it has to protect the coast fortifications. And besides, if he doesn't volunteer he may be sent to the Russian frontier, and that is a long way off."

She went silently into the kitchen and said nothing more about it. But in the fall, she gave me my clothes all whole and clean, as they should be, and mostly brand new. And she was quite contented, because Kiel is so near Itzehoe. Our storekeeper, who had relatives in Kiel, had told her, too, that many sons of good, skilled workmen serve in the marine corps.

CHAPTER 2

Peter Volunteers for Africa

I liked being a soldier, especially when we had our training behind us. We had nothing but a good sort of fellows in the room, and the subordinate officer was disagreeable only when someone was lazy or dirty. The lieutenant we did not judge rightly in those days. Afterwards, however, we learned that he was a hero. In the beginning of my second year of service, in the Christmas holidays, 1903, I was spending my furlough with my parents at Itzehoe, and I danced at a ball the night after Christmas with Marie Genthien. I had known her as a child, but had never met her since. I didn't even know that for two years she had been out to service in Holtenau Street in Kiel. When we were dancing together for the third time we laughed and said, both at the same moment, "That goes well!" We neither of us had the slightest thought that anything serious would come of it. On the day after New Year's I went back to Kiel, to my service.

Two weeks later—it was the fourteenth of January—I was walking with Behrens and another comrade through Danish Street, when Gehlsen, who was now really serving his year, and in my company, came toward us and said: "Have you read the paper?"

"What is it?" I said.

"In South West Africa the blacks, like cowards, have treacherously murdered all the farmers and their wives and children."

I am good in geography, but at first, I was completely bewildered and asked: "Are those murdered people Germans?"

"Of course," he replied, "Schlesians and Bavarians and all the other German peoples, and three or four from Holstein, too. And now what do you suppose we marines—"

Then I suddenly recognised from his eyes what he wanted to say.

"We have to go!" I said.

13

He raised his shoulder. "Who should, if not the marines?" said he.

I was silent a little while; a great deal was going through my mind. Then I was done with thinking, and I said: "Well, then we'll at it!" And I was glad.

As I went along I looked at the people who were passing, and I wondered if perhaps they knew and if they could see in us that we were going to the South West to be revenged on a heathen people for the German blood that had been spilled.

One morning it really came to the point. The major made a long speech in the courtyard of the barracks. This and that had happened out there. A regiment of volunteers was to be sent out. Who would go? Nearly all of us stepped forward. The physicians examined us to see if we were fit for service in the tropics. They found me capable of service. That same afternoon we had dealt out to us the high yellow boots and the short blue jackets or *litewkas*. Thus, equipped we went immediately into the city.

What a bowing and calling to one another there was then! Though usually soldiers who do not know one another pass without so much as a greeting, this time we were spoken to by everybody. The 85th were very reserved because they had to stay at home; the sailors spoke with dignity, as if every one of them had already travelled three times around the world. Many citizens spoke to us, too. They said it would be a very interesting journey and would be a pleasant memory for us as long as we lived, and they wished us a safe return.

The next day, when we were to take the train at night for Wilhelmshafen, father and mother came over from Itzehoe for two hours. I met them at the station and walked with them along Holsten Street as far as the Schlossplatz. My father asked all sorts of questions: whether there were wild animals there; whether the enemy all had guns, or whether they still used bows and arrows; whether it was very hot and malarial there, and such things. I couldn't answer very much to all this because I didn't know much about it. I took it for granted, however, that it was all as he said, and agreed with him in everything. We sat for an hour in a restaurant near the station, looking out of the windows at the people who were passing, but we didn't talk much. My mother hardly spoke at all. She stared at the floor with great set eyes, and, when she looked up, regarded me as though she should never see me again. When it was time I took them back to the station.

When the train for Hamburg came, and they had to get in, my father begged me to bring him home some trifle,—a horn, or some ornament worn by the enemy, or some such thing. I believe he had saved up his request so as to have something to say at the last moment. But my mother suddenly threw her arms about me and held me, weeping. As she hadn't embraced me since my earliest childhood, I was startled, and said: "What are you doing, mother?"

She replied: "I do not know whether I shall see you again, my son."

I laughed and shook her hands, saying: "There is no danger. I shall come back again." The parents of Behrens were at the station, too.

When I came back in the dark to the barracks, everything was alive there. Parents, brothers and sisters, relatives, sweethearts, and friends had come. They were dancing, drinking and talking. Among them was one old man who had worn the Iron Cross since 1870, and was now a foreman at the dock; his boy was going out with us. He stood up and spoke a few words about bravery and fidelity to the flag, just as if we were to fight a serious enemy, and we enjoyed listening to him. Yes, indeed, at his words we became all fire and flames and readily forgot that we knew we were going to fight against crossbows and clubs of wood. We wanted to fight honourably, and, if it had to be, even to die for the honour of Germany.

At midnight, the battalion formed and we marched through the city with a full band. If I live to be a hundred years old I shall never forget that hour, when thousands of people followed along with us, pressing into our ranks, calling out to us, greeting us, waving and throwing flowers at us, and carrying our arms all the way to the station. The square in front of the station was black with people.

On the journey to Wilhelmshafen I slept and dozed. The others were tired, too. When, we arrived, I went with some others into a small restaurant and bought for a great deal of money a very little poor food. At four in the afternoon we formed again and marched double-file, fully equipped, down the long narrow flight of steps leading from the quay to the deck of the ship, gazed at all the time by crowds of people gathered from all the country round. It was a clear, bitter cold, winter day.

Chapter 3

The Voyage

We went down two short flights of stairs and came into a rather large, low room, which was filled with an amazing number of beds. They were arranged close together in pairs, one above and one below. Very narrow passageways ran between them and along the wall. I got a lower berth.

We now put on our beds everything we had, our firearms, knapsacks, and clothes-bags. We packed and bustled about among our things, and from time to time looked out the portholes at the water. We were lively and in good spirits, as soldiers always are in new quarters, reminded only by the continual tremor felt throughout the ship from the motion of the engine, that these quarters were carrying us far away. We ate at long tables on one side of the same room, and that night we had pea soup and coffee.

Later I went upstairs for a little while, and stood by the rail in the lee of the first cabin and looked over to the coast. In the darkness, I saw only a yellowish, blurry glow from the ship-lights on the black, restless waves, and in the distance some motionless lights, probably those of lighthouses or lightships, and in the heavens the stars. Then I became oppressed by the thought that I should be carried off and could not help myself, and that I should have to endure all sorts of frightful things in a foreign land. I got help by swearing to God that I would be good and cheerful and brave, whatever happened to me.

The next morning, as far as the eye could reach, there was nothing but the dark, grey ocean. On the horizon, there were some clouds of smoke and some little sails. We went on deck for roll-call, and each of us got a uniform of light brown linen called khaki, and a great pot-shaped, light brown cork helmet, called a tropical helmet. We laughed and admired each other, then went to our sleeping-room and tried on our helmets amid all sorts of nonsense. After that we fastened buttons on our uniforms.

We stood a great deal at the portholes, looking out, and were occupied all day; some of us were already writing picture postcards.

Late in the afternoon I stood for a long time forward in the bow with Henry Gehlsen and talked with him about our childhood. Then some other one-year volunteers came up, among them a physician, as I afterwards learned, and began to talk to him. As they were soon talking of learned things I went off. As time went on I was often with him. He was small in stature, and had a delicate face; but he was every inch a man. Later, in the bush, he showed himself prudent, ingenious, and brave.

On the second day, we stood at the starboard rail and looked over to the coast of England, which rose mighty, steep, and rugged out of the water not far off; and we watched the fishing-boats, which, with their grey and black sails, lay in great numbers on the broad, ever-moving ocean. As I looked at this great, extended picture, I thought that in just such or even smaller vessels our forefathers had, thousands of years ago, traversed the same rough way that we now followed, straight over the waves, or rather between them, and I imagined the wild struggles that they had to go through before they had built their huts and found a home on these forbidding shores. I thought of all this, and was glad that I had had such a good teacher and that I was probably the first of all my schoolmates at Itzehoe who had seen this part of the world with his own eyes.

While I stood there the staff physician passed me, and with him the first lieutenant of the marines. They were going, probably, to visit a sailor who was sick. We had on board an officer in command of the sailors who was going out as a substitute to the Habicht. They stood a while at the railing not far from me, and I heard the first lieutenant say to the other man:

We seamen think differently about the Englishmen from the people who live inland. We meet them in all the ports of the world and we know that they are the most respectable of all the peoples. There behind the high chalk cliffs dwells the first nation of the earth,—distinguished, wise, brave, united, and rich. As for us—well, one of their qualities, bravery, we have had for ages; one other, riches, we are slowly acquiring. Whether we ever acquire the others—that is our life problem.

I wondered over that speech, but afterwards the old African settlers, whom I came to know, also spoke with the greatest respect of
the English.

The weather was cold, clear, and windy. We saw small boats tossing
up and down on the waves, but our great ship didn't roll much and
only a few of us were a little seasick. I couldn't bear to look up the
long deck and see how it slowly rose and then sank. It seemed to me
be unreasonable and unreal, and it gave me an oppressed feeling in my
head and body. It had the same effect on others, too; but when I pulled
myself together and straightened up and walked up and down, looking
out over the sea, it passed off. When we got out of the English Chan-
nel, though, opposite the realm of Spain, it suddenly got bad.

I was just standing thinking by my bed with Gehlsen near me. We
were both looking at a picture of his parents which they had given
him to take. At that moment, the floor suddenly pushed itself up diagonally under our feet, while a fearful creaking and smashing and
falling and shouting began on all sides of us. We fell over each other
onto the bed and tried in all directions to find some firm hold. With
some difficulty, we got on our feet again and clung to the iron posts
which supported the berths, while the other side of the ship went way
up against the opposite row of beds.

We tried to get away from between the rows of beds as though that
would be our salvation; but I had taken only a few steps when I began
to feel just as I did when I was twelve years old and had just smoked
my first cigar. A heavy feeling of oppression weighed on my head and
my stomach came up and up, right into my throat. My courage and
all desire to live vanished and drops of sweat fell from my forehead.
Stumbling and wretched, I went back down the passage and flung
myself on my bed. It was lucky that I didn't have to get into an upper
berth.

It was a bad night. Whenever I think of it now, after two years, it
gives me an awful feeling, and I have to swallow. My! what gagging
and vomiting on all sides! Many moaned as though their last day had
come. Just one fellow, who probably had drunk sea-water from his
nursing bottle, or in some other way had acquired the stomach of
an ostrich, laughed aloud from time to time and was cheerful and
in good spirits; just as if an angel among hordes of the damned were
laughing in its beautiful and safe blessedness.

When I woke, towards morning, out of a dull, heavy sleep, it was
somewhat smoother. Still, many were groaning. He of the cast-iron

digestion was whistling softly and comfortably. Then I was angry and scolded myself. I summoned all my will-power, and noticed the rising and falling of the ship, and thought to myself:

See! Here it goes and there it goes! It can't do otherwise, and everything on it and in it must go, too, and there is nothing to be done to prevent it. It is nonsense to buck against it. Go with it. That's it! Can't you go any further? Then back again. That's it! No further? Then back again to the other side.

Talking that way to myself, I began to feel brighter. I listened to the fellow with the cast-iron digestion and observed that in his whistling he was keeping time with the motion of the vessel.

Then I noticed that I was better and at the same time that the air in the room was horrible. I sat up in bed very deliberately and cautiously put my feet down. Three times I got on my feet and three times I sat down again. Then I went stumbling along slowly and as carefully as if I had a stomach made of thin glass, and arrived safely outside. I fell against the rail, and clung to it with both arms while I breathed the fresh air and stared dully and stupidly into the grey twilight.

And then, while I stood there, mindful of the throbbing of the ship and its heavy roll, and staring at the huge, rushing, foaming waves, I had a piece of great good luck. I saw an immense sailing-vessel gliding along not far from us. With all its monstrous sails set it lay over before the wind, so that in the grey morning light I could see the whole deck and the helmsman wrapped in a thick coat sitting comfortably on the skylight with his short pipe in his mouth. The ship rose and fell heavily and powerfully from bow to stern. Out of two of the windows came a bright glow. So, the mighty vision passed in the grey dawn, down the wild dark path of the sea, without sound or effort, beautiful, as though filled with a great, peaceful soul.

I have never seen anything more beautiful made by man. It made me well. It grew warmer now every day, not because spring was coming, but because we were going south all the time and the sun's rays fell more vertically upon us. The sea was smooth, the sun shone, and we were very busy every forenoon. A beam had been set up at the stern with a target fastened to it for us to shoot at with our new rifles. The officers shot, too, with revolvers, and each one bragged about his own weapon. Afternoons we sat about on deck cleaning our guns or washing and mending our clothes, and we talked and sang while we worked. Evenings we sat in a circle and told barrack-room stories, or each one told something about his own home. Some of them could declaim pieces that they had learned or made up. All this went on in High German, and they teased us from Holstein because, they said, we took the letter "s" between our teeth as if it were a needle. I was glad that all the natives of Schleswig-Holstein on board happened to be good, orderly men. There are, of course, even in our province, troublesome people.

We naturally talked a good deal about the near future, and it made us angry to think that the insurrection might perhaps be subdued before we arrived, and we shouldn't even leave the ship. We wanted at least to land, so that afterwards we could tell at home about the African forests, the herds of monkeys and antelopes, and the straw huts under the palms.

Some of the men played "*skat*" all the time, their enthusiasm continually waxing greater and their cards dirtier. It made no difference to them what was going on around them. They never looked up, whether we said to them, "Here, you fellows! see the flying-fishes! they are wheeling just like a squadron!" or "A big English steamer is coming!" or "Just look up and see what a fine sunset; the whole sea is gold and green and the waves have dark blue crests!" or "We see the back of a whale!" or "Have you seen the phosphorescence? just go to the stern and see the waves all full of warm, red fire"; they would just shake their heads impatiently, or say, "Go and look at it yourself," and play on. They were not playing for money.

There were quite a good many young boys among us, twenty years old or younger. I think many of them were pretty homesick. And some of them, it seemed to me, were frightened at the newness of everything they saw. Everything was so astounding to them, almost uncanny, and they got more and more silent. I used to wonder how these young, quiet ones would do if we went into a really hard war. We went afterwards into a really hard war, and every one of them made a splendid record for himself. Others sat in a corner and practiced by the hour to get up a band. One had a comb, another had clappers, a third whistled through his fingers, our musicians contributed flutes and a drum, and a little Schlesian was the leader. It was he, too, who always started the songs which we sang together every evening. There was one song we used to sing that rang out sadly far over the water: "*Nach der Heimat möcht' ich wieder!*" To this day, when I see in memory the faces of those who used to sing it, my heart stands still and I have to press my lips together.

It was getting warmer and sunnier all the time, and we had reached the entrance to the Strait of Gibraltar. We took off our blue clothes and put on our khaki things. All the time, day and night, the ship throbbed with the motion of the engine as the human body does with the beating of the heart. God knows how many times the wheels revolved.

So, we went on, always to the south, with the sea always sunny and glistening. I was astonished that the world was so big. One day I saw by the chart, which hung in the companionway, and on which our position was marked each day, that we should soon come to the island of Madeira. And indeed, very early the next day, when I went to take a look around on deck, where many were already assembled, there lay before us, not far away, a bright-coloured island.

Rough rocks rose stern and bald before us, and the middle ones wore as a crown the broad old fortifying walls. In front a rather large city, with white, flat-roofed houses, stretched itself back toward the heights at the foot of the old fortification till it was lost in luxuriant green, in forests and fields of flowers.

We were coming nearer this wonder all the time. We stood and marvelled, and glided into the bay just as curious children edge up to a picture-book, until we lay directly before the city. Then we heard shouting and calling under us, and looked down into boats close by the ship, which were filled with men looking, with their dark skins and brilliantly coloured clothes, like Italians. They stood in the boats and held up baskets of fruit and called to us; but we didn't buy anything, for we knew that we should land.

In the afternoon I went, with a lot of others, down the narrow wooden steps that were let down over the side into one of our big boats, and was rowed ashore. How novel and gay everything was! Our lieutenant had said to us in warning:

I want to say one thing to you. Don't go and buy everything you see. Not everything that is bright is beautiful or real. And look out how you drink the wine.

But it wasn't long before groups of twos and threes were standing in the low, wide-open shops buying blouses and shawls made of glistening silk, in the most lovely colours, for sisters and sweethearts. And they called to me:

You must get a souvenir to take home, Moor. Perhaps the insurrection will be over and we shan't land. If you say afterwards at home that you were with us and have nothing to show, no one will believe it.

That seemed reasonable, and I went in and bought two little silk scarfs for my two oldest sisters, for I had no sweetheart and my mother would never put on anything so bright. As we were coming out, the same lieutenant who had said so grandly, "I warn you," came by, and he already had a package in his hand. I had to laugh a little, and he did, too.

It was just as though we all, upon landing, became intoxicated with a charmed wine: everything shone in such splendid colours, the sun seemed so beautifully bright and soft, and all the people were so happy. I thought to myself: "Keep your eyes open and see what you can; who knows if you will ever again get so far away from home?"

I went through several streets and wondered over everything I saw, even over a long-eared horse that was going along in front of his truck, till I realised suddenly that it was a mule such as I had sometimes seen in pictures. I looked at the foreign words on the signs over the shops and I learned some of the names on the wares. I watched the women, with their gay head and shoulder shawls, and the men, who wore bright scarfs around their bodies, and I was surprised at the pride shown in the lines of their mouths and at the dark fire in their eyes. A soldier came along, a handsome fellow, but wearing a slovenly uniform. He raised his hand to his cap and looked at me in a friendly fashion, and I greeted him in the same way.

After I had walked about alone awhile, I came down again to the shore and found some of my comrades sitting in an open wine-room, close to the street, almost on the sidewalk. They were at little tables, zealously writing picture postcards and drinking at the same time from small glasses. I sat down with them, ordered a glass, and wrote a card to my parents. I wanted to write one to my uncle in Hamburg, but I didn't get to it. I had to look around me all the time. My mother had often scolded me for my curiosity when I used to open every box and drawer in her worktable; but when she once complained of this to my teacher, he laughed and said: "That is desire for knowledge."

After a time, some of our men came by singing noisily and reeling a little. I begged the others to go along. The landlord, in a red waistcoat and shirtsleeves, didn't know a word of German, but he did know the German money. When I saw the lieutenant standing on the quay, I was curious to know if he had bought the nice wine as well as the pretty shawls; but when I came near him I could see that his eyes were drunk only with all the beautiful gay, friendly things he had seen. For a whole day, when we were again on the ocean, I saw in a dreamy memory the handsome people walking on the gay, sunny streets, and in the background the soft hills rising in their lovely fresh fertility.

On the third morning after this I was standing, rather early, by the rail, waiting for the morning drill and looking off over the water, absorbed in thinking whether I could discover in the distance one of the Cape Verde Islands, in the neighbourhood of which we were. It seemed a useless search, for it was still misty. Then Behrens, who was standing near me, looked up suddenly, and said: "Look there! What an extraordinary white cloud that is!"

I looked up, and saw high in the sky a heavy, motionless, snow-white cloud, with a soft sheen on it like white feathers. I stood gazing and thinking, "What a wonderful cloud that is!" when Gehlsen came running forward, quick as he always was, and said, in his brisk, daring way: "Do you see it already? Look! That is the Peak of Teneriffe. It rises out of the sea to that height and its summit is white with snow in the burning glare of the sun."

I was so startled that I trembled,—it took such a hold upon me, this marvel that God had set here in the midst of the broad expanse of water under the scorching sun. We all stood and gazed, some speaking aloud, but many of us silent; and as we looked we saw the mist up there on the monstrous height part and reveal the smooth, horribly steep rocks which were piled one above another like huge old ramparts. On the topmost broad, crumbling wall lay the eternal snows, slowly we glided by the stony base.

We were still going south night and day. It is wonderful how big the world is. The hand slips easily and quickly on the map from Hamburg to Swakopmund; but how the engine works, monotonously, untiringly, day and night, for three long weeks! What strength and will men have, who are willing to go so far away to live and trade and explore and govern!

We had target practice now every morning and popped away by the hour. We drilled a little, too, and the spirit was always good. We were steering southeast to the African coast, where we were to take on board, in passing, seventy negroes, as most of the ships do which go to Swakopmund. These negroes are stokers and trimmers and helpers of all sorts on the way down, and they load and unload at Swakopmund and then go back again with the ship and are set ashore on their own coast.

On the seventh day after we passed Teneriffe, we saw the coast of Africa rising. It was just exactly as we had imagined it,—pretty huts under palms, many beautiful tall trees on gently rising slopes; and it swarmed with people. That all these people were black we could not then see.

When we were at no great distance, Gehlsen came and told me that the fathers and grandfathers of these negroes had been slaves in North America, and that the government there had brought them back to their home again and was helping them to maintain a free republic. When he had told me this, he went forward to see better, for we were getting pretty near now; but I ran down to the cabin to write a card, for the mail was going ashore. While I sat absorbed in my writing I heard such a shouting and exclaiming and stupid shrieking and such a slipping and pulling and sliding that I sprang up and went out.

I was so astonished that I stood staring with my mouth open, for over both sides were climbing like cats and writhing like snakes, the negroes, old and young men and little boys. They were tall, black, and half naked, with large exposed teeth and wild, laughing human eyes, wearing about their breasts and bodies little bright-coloured cloths and carrying sacks and pots and chests. They ran joking and laughing over the deck, quite unmindful of our amazement, and crawled down in the hold, where they established themselves. We lay to, at that place, only a few hours, and then went on again, always to the south, day after day and all through the bright nights.

On one of these days I went up to the third engineer, who was a native of Eckernford, and asked him to take me down to the engine-room. We went through many passageways and rooms which I did not even know were there, and down short iron staircases which I hadn't seen, getting deeper and deeper into the hold, where it shook more and more violently under my feet, and where I could hear the heavy movement of the great shafts and pistons more and more plainly. Then he opened an iron door and I stood before the engine. The biggest engine I had ever seen up to this time was one in a brewery in Hamburg. This one was five times as big, with pistons as long and broad as the body of a ten-year-old boy.

They swung easily in the cylinders, and the two mighty shafts, on the ends of which are the screws, revolved busily. A man in middle life, rather fat and oily, whom I had never seen before, although we had lived now three weeks on the same boat, stood quietly on a grated iron platform, which trembled violently, and looked about him in the midst of all the rising and falling and driving machinery as placidly as a farmer in a cow-barn surveys his munching herd. I went, also, carefully along the platform and down a flight of stairs through an open trapdoor, to the reddish-brown furnace-room, in which half-naked men were standing surrounded by coal, iron-barrows, and hissing valves, in front of the boilers under which the great fires glowed. I looked sharply and quickly around and would gladly have stayed longer, but I felt ashamed to be idly watching those men working so hard in the hot room.

In my free time, I used often to watch the black men, and I noticed how peacefully they sat together and talked in gurgling tones, and how they squatted around the great pots of food, stuffing quantities of rice into their mouths with their fingers, and devouring with their great, beast-like, crunching teeth their meat, bones, and all indiscriminately. It did not seem to occur to them to eat anything on account of the taste, but merely to fill their stomachs. It seemed to me like this: that the people of Madeira, although they are strangers to us, are like cousins whom we seldom see; but that these blacks are quite, quite different from us, so that there could be at heart no possible understanding or relationship between us. There must always be misunderstandings instead.

As at the beginning of the journey, we talked now a great deal about our expectations, about the palms and the monkeys we should see, and the hides and the birds and the baskets we should take home. We spoke again about the probability that the rebellion would be over before we got there.

As we came near the equator there was a lot of joking about it. Those who were a little embarrassed or dreamy were teasingly told to look out and see the line on the water, and to hold on tight when we went downhill, and all that sort of thing. I took no part in this teasing, for I am not inclined that way and I was sorry for the fellows who were the butt of it. They were, indeed, far from being stupid and thoughtless; but often those who made sport of them were the stupid and thoughtless ones who were always talking big. So, I used to draw their ridicule to myself and pretended not to see it. If I wanted to I could shake off the dogs, and I used to laugh to myself over their barking and biting. Toward evening we began to sing, and oftenest we wanted to sing the third *stanza* of a well-known song which rang out beautifully over the darkening ocean:—

Dooh mein Schicksal will es nimmer,
Durch die Welt ich wandern muss.
Trantes Heim, dein denk' ich immer . . .

At night, it was almost intolerably hot in the cabin. Some of the men scolded about it, but the more reasonable understood that it couldn't be otherwise. If anyone once woke up it was nearly impossible for him to go to sleep again. Once, when I was lying there sleepless and restless, it seemed to me that the little Schlesian—the one who liked to sing and who sang so well and whose berth was close at my right hand—sobbed aloud. When I asked what was the matter he was silent at first and then said, in a gentle, quiet voice: "This traveling is getting tiresome, don't you think so? Always, day in and day out, I don't know how many miles—it doesn't seem possible that we shall ever find our way back." Then he lay quiet again.

On the seventh day after the negroes had slipped over the rail, a sailor told us in the morning that we should reach Swakopmund that day. So, we stood by the hour at the bow, looking out; but a fog hid the coast. Toward noon, however, the fog lifted, and we saw on the horizon some great steamers and behind them an endless strip of reddish-white sand lifting itself out of the ocean. The harsh, glaring sun burned down on the dunes and sea, and we thought at first that it was a bar which lay off the shore so that the great city of Swakopmund and the palms and lions wouldn't get their feet wet; but soon, when the fog had entirely receded, we saw in the glittering light some white houses and barracks and a lighthouse on the bare sand. Then all stood amazed and delivered their opinions. Many looked silently and soberly upon the inhospitable, barren land; others jeered and said: "To come so far for a country like that!"

We were not disembarked that day. Some said we weren't going ashore at all, that the revolt had already been put down; others said that it would last a long while yet. There was great uneasiness and talking back and forth among us. Flag signals were energetically exchanged until nightfall between us and the cruiser Habicht. We lay that night, rocking in a pretty heavy swell, off Swakopmund.

CHAPTER 4

By Railway to the Capital

Very early the next morning we got over the rail and climbed in order down the rope-ladder to the great flatboat which rose and sank certainly seven yards on the heavy waves. Each man had his knapsack and his white sleeping blanket on his back, his gun on his shoulder, his cartridge-belt, from which hung the water-sack, around his waist, and his bread-bag and army flask hanging from a strap. We had to look out that we let go the rope-ladder at just the right time, when the boat was on the crest of a wave; but although I did it right I fell heavily against the gunwale. When the flatboat had twenty or thirty men in it, it was fastened to a little low tugboat and we were towed to land.

The nearer we came to the shore the rougher became the water. The boat flung itself more and more violently through surging, leaping surf. We lay often between two billows which ran so high that we couldn't see anything of the steamer in front of us. The next moment we were on top of a wave and thought we should be pitched down into the trough. At last we went through mere froth and foam, which leaped high around us and threw spray over us till we were wet through and through. For a time, the boat was so pounded up and down on the heavy, choppy waves that I thought it would be dashed to pieces. Many of the men were taken suddenly and violently seasick and lay deathly pale on the bottom of the boat. But after a while we got out of that part into smooth water and went ashore.

Through everlastingly deep, hot sand, under a scorching sun, with about sixty pounds apiece on our backs, we marched inland. We had thought that all Swakopmund would be standing on the beach, overjoyed that help had at last arrived; but not a single human being was there. We passed isolated houses which stood there on the bare sand, but not a soul showed himself to offer us a friendly greeting. When we chanced to get sight of any one nearby or far off in the shadow of a veranda, it seemed to us that he looked at us indifferently and even scornfully. Behind us we could hear the pounding of the surf,—it already sounded almost lovely to us,—and around us as far as we could see there was nothing but barren, hot sand, on which the sun burned with a hard glare. We could hardly keep our eyes open, and a hot, dry feeling cramped our throats. We were pretty quiet.

We reached the big sandy station and watched our train with astonishment and mistrust as it drew in, rattling and creaking. It was made up of an endless string of little rough sand-cars, in front of which were attached five or seven tiny engines. We were divided among the cars and got in. Then, amid puffing and joggling and rattling, the train started slowly toward the interior.

We went up grade all the time, hour after hour. As far as we could see ahead and on both sides, there was nothing but yellowish white sand dunes, which sometimes rose to a great height. We stood and squatted and sat tightly crowded in the little open cars. As the oppressive heat made us thirsty all the time, we were continually and improvidently opening our water-sacks. We were just as improvident in throwing away the coffee we had brewed in the station at Swakopmund when we tasted it and found it had got sour. Once or twice we stopped in order to limber up our legs, which were lame with standing or sitting. Late in the afternoon the grade became so steep that the train was divided into three sections, so that, part by part, it could get up the steep heights. As we all pushed, this was accomplished without accident. Then we went along somewhat faster again, still through the yellow sand dunes and still up hill all the time.

In the evening, we reached the top of the ascent. Behind us the yellow, sandy road descended to the sea, about twenty-five miles in the distance. Right before us stood a monstrous, horribly wild mountain range. I had never seen mountains. Not only I myself and the other North Germans, but also the Bavarians were amazed at the sight. Quite close in front of us and also receding into the distance, huge naked rocks rose to the sky. Some were lighted up by the evening sun and shone bright and hard; others, gloomy and fearful, hung menacing, often directly over us. On all sides were evidences of the mighty powers that had ruled of old, that had knocked off pieces of rock and precipitated them into the depths, and had left other pieces, already split away, hanging at a frightful height, as though they might plunge down at any moment. Little powers could not exist here. We didn't see a shrub or even a spear of grass, and not an animal. We, the only living beings, were rolling along through this immense, dead wonderwork, on our little creaking cars, ridiculous to look upon.

We stopped at a little station, a house made of corrugated sheet iron, and boiled some coffee and rice for ourselves. When we got on board again we were ordered to take the barrel-covers off our guns and to load. I did it with a very disagreeable feeling. We proceeded amid loud confusion, which resounded harshly and hideously into the light grey night. We were passing along a deep, narrow valley between high rocks on both sides. Many of us were crouching, drunk with sleep; some were standing, others sitting on the edge of the car; everyone had his white woollen blanket around him. We didn't say much.

Many were probably at home in thought or saw themselves coming home and telling of all the wonders they had seen. Many, very likely, were thinking how the enemy could shoot down from every rock upon our little handful of men, while we slowly passed by, almost defenceless. So, we brooded, weary, hungry, and all used up. In the broad, clear sky numberless twinkling stars shone out of a bright blue ground. That was indeed a beautiful, sublime picture. Still it was not as beautiful nor as impressive nor as peaceful as in my native land. We travelled all night, and it was disagreeably cold.

During the greater part of the next day, which again was hot and sunny, we were still passing through the valleys of that horrible, bare mountain range. As we thought we should be able to refill our water-sacks at one of the next stations, we drank until our supply was gone. But when at noon we really did stop at a station for the engine to take in water, and we were permitted to take water for ourselves, we could not drink it, for it was repulsively salt. By that time, we were out of bread, too. We boiled a handful of our rice half tender and ate it, and we cleaned out our utensils a little with sand. Then we went on. Many a one seized upon the strong potion which he had in his knapsack, although it was forbidden to touch it. But thirst was much worse than hunger. We had no moisture in our mouths to wet our lips a little. Our breath came dry and hot through our parched mouths, and the burning dryness penetrated, as though with spurs and prickles, ever deeper into our throats.

In the afternoon, we emerged at last from the mountains into a wide plain. We stretched our necks as far as we could when we came out, for we thought, now that we had finally left behind us, first the rising dunes and then the wild mountains, that groves of palms must appear. But what we saw was a broad plateau of reddish yellow earth, sparsely grown with coarse, yellow, dry grass, which waved like rye as high as a man's knee. In the grass were scattered, at first thinly, then more thickly, tough, thorny bushes, ranging from the height of a man to three or four yards. At last they were so close together that their tops touched one another.

In the distance, we suddenly saw isolated cones of mountains, rising, here and there, abruptly out of the broad plain. Once or twice we saw before us in the far, far distance, raised a little from the plain and glistening in the hot, trembling air, that which we longed to see,—high, fruitful trees and blue surfaces like ponds. But they vanished again; they were mirages.

Although we were far from being pleased with what we saw, we were in a somewhat better mood. There was always something to be seen. A strange, deer-like animal chased in herds through the long, waving, yellowish grass; or an unfamiliar, brilliantly coloured bird flew up. The pointed mountain cones stood out sharply in the sun, and we saw plainly on their slopes or at their bases jagged heaps of stones which had slid down from the heights. As we advanced, the grass and bushes got a little softer and the prospect a little more pleasing. Everything we saw, whether near or far, was sharply outlined in the wonderfully clear air.

We had become rather more cheerful, in spite of our thirst, when we arrived at the first stopping-place which the negroes had destroyed. They had burned out the modest house, torn down the tin roof, smashed the little household furniture, and taken everything else with them. In the meagre little garden, where one could still see traces of the care with which German hands had tended it, lay a heap of white stones. There, buried three feet deep in the barren soil, lay the settler and his wife, who had been attacked and killed by the negroes. The five or six sailors from the Habicht, who at the time held possession of the place, had nailed together a cross out of pieces of boxes and had written upon it with a dull pencil the names of the killed and the words, "Fallen by the hand of the murderer." The windows they had fortified with tin cement tubs and with sacks full of sand.

The sailors were very serious and quiet. Their uniforms were dirty and entirely spoiled. One of them stepped up to the car in which I sat, and said: "You'll find a good deal of work to do still. We haven't been out of our clothes for three weeks."

I said: "We know very little; what is the state of things?"

"What is the state of things?" he repeated. "We have had heavy losses."

"Dead?" asked one of our number.

"Dead!" said the sailor, surprised. "In the last weeks, we have lost more than forty dead. They shoot well and with good guns,—with those, in fact, sold them by us, or taken from our magazines, or off our dead."

"Is that so?" we said.

"I wish you all may get back to your mothers," he said.

The day's journey was again long and thirsty, and we were completely exhausted. Toward evening we came to a larger station, and slept on the ground, wrapped in our blankets with our knapsacks under our heads, in barracks built of corrugated iron. When I awoke, early, before dawn, my next neighbour, a little quiet Thuringian, noticed it and said to me in a low voice: "I don't know what will happen if I never get home again. I am the eldest, with five brothers and sisters, and my father is sickly. When he dies I must be there to take care of all the others."

"You will get home, all right," said I.

"I must," he replied.

Then he lay still, and when I turned my head a bit to one side he was looking up with wide-open eyes. I don't believe he saw the tin roof at which he gazed, but instead he saw the living-room and the barn of his parental home.

That morning, when I was walking about the station building, I saw the first of the enemy, a prisoner and his wife. He was a tall man with a strong, proud body, half-naked, with a vacant, indifferent expression in his passive but dismal face. The woman was elderly and very ugly. At noon, the next day we continued the journey through the same flat land, which was now, however, somewhat more fertile and had long yellow grass, and bushes, and even occasional trees growing on it; but everything was still dried up and of a greyish green colour. The stations we now passed were almost all destroyed, and near many a one lay a heap of white stones which indicated a grave.

In the middle of the night we reached a great station building, the windows of which had been walled up into loopholes. In three or four sheds of corrugated iron a lot of provisions had been piled up. In the square court of a fortification which was there we had at last a real meal,—pea soup, and meat and rice.

On the next day, the fourth and last of our journey, the country became more fruitful and more attractive. Nearby and in the distance groups of tall trees which looked like oaks were to be seen from time to time in the high grass. Among them ran a broad strip of yellow sand, the dried-up bed of a river. There for the space of three days in December of the year before waves had danced along, leaving traces still to be seen in the sand; but now it was entirely dry, and would stay so for a year, and perhaps for three. It was just so with all the rivers we had come across in this country; they were strips of sand half a yard or a yard lower than the plain.

I rather liked the landscape through which we passed on this fourth day. Two kinds of antelopes, a smaller and a larger, like deer, would sometimes run alone, or in herds, across the bare places in the brush. Strange grey-and-white-speckled birds, somewhat bigger than partridges, flew over the bushes and down again. Clumps of beautiful, stately trees stood in the midst of the soft green, and from a distance the green mountain slopes formed a far from unpleasing sight. But my comrades didn't like the country; I think it wasn't strange and wonderful enough for them. They wanted Africa to look entirely different in every particular from their native land.

In the afternoon, we reached the capital city. It was small, spread out, and quite irregularly built. Here and there on the sandy grey earth were flat-roofed white houses, among which stood occasional sorry-looking trees. We panted under our heavy packs through sand and sun up to the fort, which was situated on a moderately high hill, and there in the courtyard, which was full of life, we broke ranks.

What a life it was that we now entered upon! For four days, we hadn't had our clothes off or washed ourselves, and for three days we hadn't had a really good swallow of water. Here in the wall of the courtyard were faucets with warm, almost hot water from the mountain running out of them. How quickly we got our clothes off and how joyfully we washed, and played the water over ourselves! How quickly we forgot our thirst and dirt! And how curiously we looked about us!

The home guards were going about in their cord uniforms: brown velvet coats, full trousers and riding-boots, and soft grey hats. Most of them had already been for years in the country. Sick or wounded, or detailed to accompany us to the enemy, as guides, they were walking back and forth, some idle and some occupied. We talked to them while we were washing ourselves, and asked them how matters stood. They were somewhat stiff, as old campaigners are, especially if one asks them all sorts of silly questions, as some of us did. However, when I addressed one of them, a sergeant, with intelligence and respect, he told me of the enemy's cruelty toward the farmers, of the heavy losses in the last fight, and of the position of the enemy. The sergeant was a Hamburg man named Hansen. Just then a lot of our men came up.

There were some women captives in the yard of the fort, and some of them were young and not ugly; but most of them were faded and hideous. They took washing to do for the soldiers, and lounged about with short pipes in their mouths, and were very dirty. I didn't like it that some of our men went right up to them and joked with them by means of signs and some English and Low-German words.

There were Boers there, too, stately, brown, long-bearded men in khaki or cord uniforms. The German government had engaged them as wagoners. Strong four-wheeled wagons, called Cape wagons, covered with linen hoods, stood outside in front of the court. These wagons were to go out with us next day and drag provisions and fodder for us into the wilderness.

We slept that night in the yard of the fort. Before I went to sleep I thought for a long time of my parents, and of Itzehoe, and of my life up to now. It came to me that it was probably more than a whole year since I had said my prayers, and I resolved to begin again.

CHAPTER 5

The Journey Inland on Foot

The next morning, while it was still dark, we broke camp. We were to surround the enemy to the northeast in a great arc, so that they couldn't escape into English territory with their own and their stolen herds of cattle. For the present, only one company with four small cannon was marching; the others were to follow in a few days.

Our guides, the home guards, went on ahead, mounted on pretty good shaggy horses, their guns resting in leather pockets on the right leg. They were for the most part old African settlers, farmers, who had been called out as militiamen. Next rode the captain with the officers. Then came the long row of wagons and the artillery.

The great wagons, drawn by long teams of oxen, rumbled clumsily along. Now the high, heavy wheels would grind into the deep sand; now a wheel would climb up on a stone lying in the rut and would fall back into position while the wagon creaked and groaned in every part. Black drivers ran alongside, calling to each ox by name and cracking the enormous whips which they held in both hands. Behind each wagon, which with its team was perhaps fifty yards long, marched a division, in dust and sand (when possible just outside the wagon track), with guns slung over their shoulders and cartridge-belts around their waists.

Single horsemen, officers, rode along at intervals near us. Last came the so-called rear guard, half a platoon. The country was for the most part covered with more or less dense brush as tall as a man. So, we proceeded in an everlastingly long train along a road which was indicated only by old and new wagon-tracks. From time to time a wagon stopped because the harness of the oxen had got out of order, or because a wheel had sunk too deep into a rut, or because an ox had collapsed and had to be unharnessed.

34

Already, on this first day, the sun shone dry and hot. The road was quite hilly and full of unevennesses besides. At eleven o'clock, when the heat was becoming unbearable, we fortunately reached a beautiful shady place, where we halted. Not far from here a fine, stately farmhouse had been totally ruined by the blacks: the windows had been torn out; the heavy, well-made furniture had been smashed to pieces; and many books were strewn about, soiled and torn. We boiled, each mess company for itself, a little rice for dinner, and lay down to rest in the shade of the wagons. In the afternoon we went on, marching till late in the evening.

In a clearing, we formed a camp and fortified it by stationing the wagons in a square around it. Besides that, we built, about fifty yards outside the wagons, at each of the four points of the compass, a little crescent-shaped barricade of bush with the big curve pointing out. In each barricade were placed an under officer and three men. The officer had to stand in the middle of the barricade, with two of the men lying diagonally back of him, and the third man had to walk back and forth through the bushes to the next barricade, a distance of about four hundred yards. It was known that many of the enemy were in the vicinity.

I belonged for the night to post number two, and lay until eight o'clock on the ground behind the under officer, and listened, my gun at hand. From a distance, out of the bush came the howling of strange wild animals. It began soft and low and grew higher and hoarser. Between whiles resounded another sort of howl, coarser and more jerky. Now and then a dry branch cracked. Is it the sentry returning from the other post? Is it the enemy? Is it an animal? The sentry comes up slowly and cautiously. He bends down a little and reports, in a low tone, inside the barricade, "Back from patrol. All clear." It was a very dark night.

Shortly afterwards it became my turn to walk up and down till morning. I got up and groped carefully along, often standing still and straining my ears toward the dark bushes surrounding me. When I came to the next post, I reported and came back the same way. Often, I thought surely that a dark body was cowering there somewhere by a bush in the grass. My heart beat wildly. A branch broke behind me. I retreated with light, careful tread, so that I had a bush at my back, and watched attentively on all sides. When all was quiet again I went cautiously on. My eyes turned hastily this way and that like mice in a trap.

On my third trip, a shot fell in front of me in the direction of the next post. The short report pierced the still darkness of the night. I fell on one knee, raised my gun, and waited till I should see an object to aim at. As I lay there the men ran out of the wagon fort to the aid of the post. I heard their voices; then their shots flashed at one side of me. The whole camp was in motion; I heard commands and hot firing. I lay and waited certainly half an hour or more and did not fire, for I saw nothing to aim at. Then it was still.

I rose and went on slowly and cautiously, that I might not be accidentally taken for an enemy and be shot. I reached the barricade safely and reported. There was only one man there. I asked him softly where the others were. He replied just as quietly that they had gone out at the first shot to help the men who were attacked, and had not returned. Then I went back again.

So, I wandered back and forth in the quiet night as I had been told to do, and each time I came to the other post I stooped and looked into the barricade and found always only the one man, who stood erect, his gun on his arm, and peered into the darkness. When I asked him softly, "The others?" he turned his head quickly toward me, raised his hand warningly, and looked out again into the night without saying a word. Then I thought that there had been some mishap.

I went up and down till the darkness began to grow greyer and greyer, and little voices began to chirp in the bushes, and in the east the morning light began to mount in five rosy stripes. Then came the relief for the sentries.

When I came into camp and was going to my mess division, who were sitting around the hole where they had their fire, and I was looking casually about me,—for the whole picture was new to me, the great heavy wagons, the old Africans in high boots and shirtsleeves around their fire-holes, the two tents of officers, the black drivers squatting in a corner, talking and laughing,—and was about to open my mouth and ask cheerfully and braggingly: "Well, what was the firing about last night?"—just at that moment the whole camp suddenly stood up and looked with earnest, wide-open eyes toward one end, where many soldiers were gathering and gazing down at the ground. And someone said: "You see? There it is."

I knew then what had happened. I went with them to where the crowd was,—and my feet were very heavy,—and there I saw three comrades lying on the ground, their breasts bloody, their mouths open, and their eyes staring and dull. A subordinate officer who had come up behind me said: "Those are the men from post number three." We

36

stood and looked down upon them. More joined the crowd. We did not speak a word. An officer came and sent us away.

Some hours later the dead, wrapped in their woollen blankets, were buried on a little hill. Eight men shot into the air over their open grave in their honour. The captain said the *Lord's Prayer*. Then we sat silent and depressed around our cooking-holes.

We stayed three or four days in this place, for orders had come for us to wait here for the major, who was following with the other company. We had to have a lot of drill; musketry practice, practice in bush fighting, and the like. Moreover, our cooking made a good deal of work, for we were awkward and unnecessarily particular about it. Every mess—there were in each at most six men—made itself as fine a cooking-hole as possible, and with much skill and much more talk, dug a knee-deep gutter in a circle around it, into which each of us could stick his feet, so that we could sit quite comfortably. Some of the mess companies prided themselves mightily on such earthworks.

Then one fellow—and it had to be one with a good grip and the gift of gab—had to fetch the rations from the wagons: rice, meat, wheat flour, salt, and coffee. Others had to collect dry wood from the bush around the camp, and still others had to fetch water from deep water-holes in the steep, black rocks. Thus, everyone had his share of the work.

One difficult matter was bread-baking. One of us remembered this, and one that; and everyone knew something about it. Some looked thoughtfully at the ground, and then getting a lucky inspiration would pour forth what had come to them. One, a native of Holstein, apparently had spent the greater part of his childhood standing near his mother in front of the oven, which was in a corner of the garden by the wall; and he even asserted that his mother had several times inadvertently set him on the shovel and pushed him into the oven. He knew, therefore, not only how it feels to be a bread-baker, but also to be the loaf of bread. He was a rogue, and we didn't listen to him.

We were very anxious to learn. The sour bread, especially, caused us much thought; but after long and heated discussion and much running to and from other divisions, we made bread of rum and flour. Some stood waiting, with shirtsleeves rolled up, ready to knead it. One advised that they should wash their hands first, and he got a sharp hint that he had made a ridiculous suggestion. There was no water for washing hands. They kneaded the dough industriously and laid it carefully in the cooking-pan over a gentle fire. It rose a little, and browned a little, but even then, it was sticky and not properly baked.

Evenings we sat around the dying fire and talked over the position of the enemy and the progress of the campaign,—for wild and wonderful rumours were current at times,—and we reverted always to the last fight. We talked of how we had found not a single dead enemy and of the possibility that our three killed had been shot by our own men, and we shook our heads and gazed into the embers; and then someone would stoop and stir up the fire a little. Next, we got to talking of Kiel and of home, and each one told something about his life or his childhood and praised it. The Swabians, especially, talked a great deal, and talked big about what they had and what they could do. Then we lay down just as we were sitting, in a circle about our cooking-hole, and pulled our blankets over us and slept.

On the fourth evening, when it was already dark and we were sitting around the fires, we saw flashes of light in the east. Immediately afterwards, it flashed in the west also. We became very much excited; we thought the enemy were giving signals about attacking us. The light hovered a moment like a white star on the horizon and then vanished and appeared again immediately. It seemed quite near. The next morning Gehlsen told me that the signals had been from our own men, who were situated in a fortification in the far east in the midst of the enemy. They had signalled way over us to the west to the capital and had received an answer from there.

Very early the next morning, the fifth, our outposts saw the major advancing. Many of us climbed on the wagons and watched the long procession, which wound slowly up out of the ravines of the mountains; and we talked as if we were already old Africans, although we were merely four days and three dead ahead of them. And one of us said to another, "The old fellow is surprised. Marching here is different from in Kiel." So, we stood and watched, and were especially pleased when we recognised the old officer. For the first time, we were superior to him.

CHAPTER 6

Brothers, or Slaves?

We were to surround the enemy in an arc to the north and corner them, just as one runs in a circle and corners a colt so that it runs back where the boy is waiting with a halter in his hand. We were to make forced marches with fewer and lighter wagons, which meant smaller and lighter rations, and with less and lighter clothing. We were about three hundred men,—marines, sailors, and the home guards, who were leading us.

The troop of old Africans again went on ahead, officers and common soldiers, all mounted. Then came the old major with one officer; then we foot-soldiers in a long, thin line veiled in dust. Here and there in our line were the thirty great Cape wagons, loaded with the light fieldpieces and each drawn by from ten to twenty-four long-horned oxen, which were driven, with much shouting, by negroes. On both sides of the way was more or less dense, greyish green thorn-bush, the wood of which is as hard as bone, and which grows to the height of a man, and sometimes twice that height, and has curved thorns as long as one's finger.

In such wise and through such country we now travelled day after day and week after week. And day by day and week by week our progress became more painful. For soon came the time when we began to suffer from hunger and want, when the oxen began to fall from exhaustion, and when some of the clumsily rumbling wagons were full of the distress of the wounded or very sick.

When the sun mounted high over us, almost to the zenith, and the sand was scorching, and eyes and throats were burning, the van would halt at a clearing where there ought to have been water, but the water was not always there. Then suffering terribly from thirst, we had to dig holes to see if we could find a little water slowly filtering through.

Often it was salt or milky from lime, or smelled vile; and oftener we didn't find even this miserable, loathsome water, and we had to go on again thirsty, far into the night. If we did find water, we would make a barricade of thorn-bush around us. Then each mess division would get its meagre supply of food; a little meat from a freshly killed ox which had fallen exhausted, a little flour, and a little rice. The meat or flour we stirred up in a kettle with the bad water, and set it over the fire, calling it meat soup, or *bouillon* with rice, or pancakes, which they called "*Plinsen*." The cooking utensils were cleaned with sand. After that we lay for an hour in the shade of the wagons or of a canvas that had been set up, and then started on again.

Weary and indifferent, we marched on till evening and often into the night, and I don't know that in those weeks we ever sang. The moonlight lay wonderfully pale, like bright spider webs, over the broad, bushy land, and the unfamiliar stars gleamed strangely confused and restless. The gun-straps pressed on our shoulders, our feet stumbled in the uneven track, and our thoughts were slow and dull. When we had reached water in the night and had had dealt out to us one or two, or, if it was more plenty, even three cook-pan covers full of the miserable stuff, we were too tired to cook properly. We stirred up together a little of whatever we got and ate it half cooked. We had orders to bring the water to the boiling-point before we took it; but I have seen the officers, and for that matter even the physicians themselves, drink it just as it was. We were too tired and apathetic.

So, it went on every day for four weeks. The country was always flat and bushy. We didn't see a single house and we didn't meet a human being.

It was bad that we couldn't take provisions enough with us. If we had been able to, many more would have seen their homes again. We didn't notice it ourselves, but the doctors and officers probably saw that we were gradually getting flabby and weak. If we had even had time and inclination to cook properly, it would have been better; but the water was often so repulsive that it was no pleasure, and we had to use it so sparingly that our utensils got foul. I rubbed them with sand and I rubbed them with grass, but they did not get clean. And it was bad that we had only thin khaki uniforms. In the morning, we marched up to our knees in wet grass, at noon in hot sand, and all day through thorny brush, so that the lower part of our trousers fringed out and soon hung in shreds. When, as sometimes happened, a thunder-storm or a shower came up and then night came on, we were horribly cold. There were some very cold nights.

Thus, it had to come about that we soon became very weak, even though we did not notice it ourselves. I used to think sometimes with surprise, "There was so much talk and squabbling among us on ship-board, and so many jokes among us! Where are they, and why don't we sing? How pale and yellow and thin Behrens has grown! How sunken and feverish our under-officer's eyes look! What awfully thin beards we young men have!" There were many among us not yet twenty.

Once we came upon a great covered wagon left deserted on the road. A farmer or a trader had wanted to escape and had packed his most valuable possessions in the wagon, harnessed his oxen to it, and driven the rest of his flocks before it. He had come as far as this. His bones lay eaten by beasts, his goods were stolen, and round about the wagon were strewn the only things which the enemy couldn't use, his letters and books. We buried the bones in the bush, tied a cross together with string and set it on the grave, and took some letters and remnants of books, read them, and threw them away.

Another day we discovered, hidden in the bush, on a hill by the way, many deserted huts of the enemy. They were like great beehives made of a skeleton of branches and twigs plastered over with cow-dung. Although we were so tired, we took the time to set fire to these, and afterwards stood on a rise in our road and looked back. The glow dyed the evening sky for a great distance.

Besides this I don't know that anything special happened to us. We marched continually along the sandy road in a cloud of dust, on both sides of us brush that from time to time was thinner, or that yielded to make a majestic clearing.

Our horsemen, the old Africans and the officers, rode often an hour in advance of us and tried to spy out the enemy. When they came back the news would often spread through the ranks or at night from fire to fire: "We are close to the enemy now; tomorrow or the day after we shall meet them." Then we rejoiced and each man sat and looked over his gun and examined his cartridge-belt. But a new day came and still another, and we grew weaker and more exhausted, and we saw nothing of the enemy.

So, it went on for four weeks, further and further. It was bad that we never had our clothes off and could never wash ourselves, and seldom, and then not thoroughly, even our faces and hands; but what was worse, we could never get enough to eat any more. They had given to me the task of getting the rations for our mess. I brought less and less to the cooking-hole; a little rice, a little flour, a little canned meat, and a little coffee. There was no more sugar, and one day I came back from the wagon with no salt. Then I baked pancakes made of dirty water and flour. The water we drank with our food tasted disgustingly of *Glaubersalz*; often it was as yellow as pea soup and smelled vile. The nights were cold.

I cannot say that we were cast down. We didn't grumble, either. We perceived that it couldn't go any other way and that the officers endured all that we did. We were very quiet and sober, though. We held ourselves together with the thought:

> We shall soon now come upon the enemy and beat them and finish up the campaign, and then, oh! then, we shall go back to the capital and get new clothes and have a bath. We'll spring into the water, and we'll get a new handkerchief, a really clean, red checked one, and a great lot of good meat and a handful of white salt, and a great, great mug of clean, crystal-clear water—how it will glisten! And we'll have a long, long drink and hold out the empty mug, and again the water will pour into it, and we'll drink and drink. And then after a few days we'll travel back to the coast and we'll start for home! What shan't we have to tell about this monkey-land!

Our boots fell apart; our trousers were nothing but shreds and rags at the bottom; our jackets got full of great holes from the thorns and were horribly greasy because we wiped everything off on them; our hands were full of inflamed places because we often had to seize the thorns with them.

Our lieutenant often talked to us. "Keep up your courage," he would say; "we shall have a fight and throw the rascals back to the west into the jaws of the main division. And in July we'll be at home again."

I marvelled at him, that he, though not much older than we, and suffering all the hardships that we did, was always uniformly calm, while we were often good-for-nothing and got angry and grumbled. It wasn't because he had learned more than we; I think it came from the fact that he was at heart a cultivated man; that is, he had his soul and mind in control so that he could value justly, and could make allowance for the things about him. His will would have it so; and it came to pass. And I have noticed that will power is worth ten times more than mere knowing. We never said a word of how much we thought of him and watched him. He was a small man and rode a strong East Prussian horse, and always wore his felt hat a little over the left ear with the brim tilted up on the left side.

The old major came sometimes and addressed us. While doing so he looked at each man as closely as though he wanted to find out if he were having any sort of trouble. We all felt that he was a wise and wide-awake man and that he had a gentle, sympathetic heart. We felt, therefore, safe under him, and we knew it could not be any different from what it was or he would have changed it; and we would run like so many rabbits if we could do any little service for him. When any one had run that way, we used to jeer at him and say: "Are you trying to burst yourself, man?" But when the turn came to anyone else he would run just the same.

Sometimes when we were all sitting about our fire-holes, I would take myself off over to the old Africans, who always had their fire by one of the wagons which Sergeant Hansen conducted. Then Hansen would motion to me, for he liked me since I had talked to him in the courtyard of the fort. They always sat by themselves, not entirely out of pride, but also because they were mostly from five to twenty years older than we were. Some of them had been already ten years or more in the country.

I used to sit down quietly with them and listen with great eagerness to their talk. Sometimes they talked of the wild fifteen years' struggles in the colony, in all or part of which they had shared, and of the fighting in the last three months. They recalled the scene of many a brave deed, and named many a valiant man, dead or living. I was surprised that so many hard undertakings, of which I had never heard or read so much as a word, had been carried through by Germans, and that already so much German blood had been lavishly spilled in this hot, barren land. They touched, too, upon the causes of the uprising; and one of the older men, who had been long in the country, said:

Children, how should it be otherwise? They were ranchmen and proprietors, and we were there to make them landless workingmen; and they rose up in revolt. They acted in just the same way that North Germany did in 1813. This is their struggle for independence.

"But the cruelty?" said someone else, and the first speaker replied indifferently:

Do you suppose that if our whole people should rise in revolt against foreign oppressors it would take place without cruelty?

And are we not cruel toward them?

They discussed, too, what the Germans really wanted here. They thought we ought to make that point clear.

The matter stood this way: there were missionaries here who said: 'You are our dear brothers in the Lord and we want to bring you these benefits; namely, Faith, Love, and Hope.' And there were soldiers, farmers, and traders, and they said: 'We want to take your cattle and your land gradually away from you and make you slaves without legal rights.' Those two things didn't go side by side. It is a ridiculous and crazy project. Either it is right to colonise, that is, to deprive others of their rights, to rob and to make slaves, or it is just and right to Christianise, that is, to proclaim and live up to brotherly love.

One must clearly desire the one and despise the other; one must wish to rule or to love, to be for or against Jesus. The missionaries used to preach to them, 'Ye are our brothers,' and that turned their heads. They are not our brothers, but our slaves, whom we must treat humanely but strictly. These ought to be our brothers? They may become that after a century or two. They must first learn what we ourselves have discovered,—to stem water and to make wells, to dig and to plant corn, to build houses and to weave clothing. After that they may well become our brothers. One doesn't take any one into a partnership till he has paid up his share.

One old freight-carrier, who mixed many English and Dutch words in his speech, said it would be better if the colony were sold to the English. "The Germans are probably useful as soldiers and farmers," he said, "but they understand nothing about the government of colonies. They want this and they want that."

A younger man, who had been in the country only three years, said, in answer: "There'll have to be a thousand or two German graves in this country before that happens, and perhaps they'll be dug this year."

Over these conversations it got to be late at night; the fires still glowed a little, and in the uncertain light I saw the faces that had become browned and weather-beaten from the burning of the African sun.

In these hard, hot days of marching and cold, moonlight nights, when we were advancing painfully, but still not without courage, one week after another, through the wild, bushy land,—there was not a house, not a ditch, not a tree, not a boundary in the burning sun by day or the pale moonlight of the clear nights; when I was plodding along, hungry and dirty and weary by the sandy, uneven wagon track, my gun on my shoulder; when I lay in the noon hour in the shadow of the great Cape wagons, and in the bitter cold nights, hungry and restless, in a thin blanket on the bare earth, and the strange stars shone in the beautiful blue heavens,—then, I believe, even then, in those painful weeks, I learned to love that wonderful, endless country.

CHAPTER 7

Peter is Promoted

Toward the end of the fourth week some horsemen, who had been
sent on ahead, came in with the report that the enemy were close by;
so, we made a better camp than usual. We set up the old major's tent
under a big tree, made a strong barricade of thorn-bush around us,
established outposts, and slept for the night. Early the next morning,
when I was coming from guard duty, I heard that all our horsemen,
not only the old Africans but also most of the officers, were to go out
as a scouting party and ascertain the position of the enemy. Soon after
that I saw that they were saddling and harnessing oxen to the one
two-wheeled wagon and the machine-gun. Then they started out of
camp, in all about forty mounted men. The major, with his straight
little figure and his searching glance, rode in the midst of them, as did
our lieutenant. I was vexed that he had taken the corporal with him
instead of me. Still, I gazed after him till the narrow sandy path disappeared in the bushes. He was wearing his hat over his left ear.

After they left, we began a grand wash, for in this place there was
quite a lot of water in deep holes which had been dug in the bright
grey limy earth. We made a broad ditch by our fire-hole, spread a
water-tight tent-cloth over it, poured water into it, took off our rags
and washed and scrubbed them with great zeal. Then we hung them
up on bushes to dry. In this way, we spent the day rather more cheerfully than for a long time, and we talked of our cavalry and when they
would come back. Toward evening I went to our commissariat wagon
and got the share for our mess and made a flour mush; and we sat
about our cooking-hole, as usual, and ate.

While we were sitting there we suddenly saw that the next mess
division were stretching their necks and getting up. At the same time,
we heard shouting from the other end of the camp. We sprang up and

saw galloping toward us, on the same path which our scouting party had taken in the morning, a single rider. He was so exhausted by his exertions that he swayed from side to side with every leap of his horse, and the horse was shiny with sweat and bespattered with foam. They helped him dismount, but he either could not or would not speak. The captain came out of his tent and led him away with him.

At that moment two more riders, old Africans, came in, one shortly behind the other. One was a native of Schleswig, a capable, earnest man. They called to the captain without dismounting and said, in a thick voice: "More than half are dead."

Then we all called out together: "Who is dead? What? Who is left? Where's the old man? Is Peter dead? Is our lieutenant dead? Speak, can't you?" But they said nothing. Then the first one came out of the tent and said: "The cart will come immediately with several officers who have been wounded."

We got our guns ready, strengthened our outposts, and sent out an expedition to meet the wagon, and waited, brooding and talking in low voices. We felt as though we had been struck on the head.

Soon we heard from a distance out of the bush the cracking of whips; then we saw the white canvas top of the wagon shimmering through the bushes. The harness of the oxen was in disorder and several of them were wounded. On the chest in the middle of the wagon sat the wounded officers; several others lay near them as though dead. The old major, however, stood upright in their midst. His hair was bloody and his face was pale. The hospital aids came running with woollen blankets, covered those who were lying in the wagon and carried them away. Blood trickled in great drops from the tail-board. After considerable time, fifteen more men came in one by one, among them Sergeant Hansen. That was all that came back.

I went over to my mess and sat there awhile despondently. The old Africans were sitting not far from us, but I did not venture to go to them, for they had become a small company. At last, however, I went and seated myself silently a little at one side.

"He wanted to come back," Sergeant Hansen was saying, staring into the fire, "but he had a bad shot in his leg, so he had to stay lying there."

Another man was mentioned. "He had luck," said the man from Schleswig. "He got a shot in the breast and lay quite still."

I asked in a low voice for our lieutenant.

"I don't know," said one.

The other one said: "He went into cover in the bush and Karl saw him fall there."

One of them told of the old major: "As long as I live, I shall hear his placid voice amidst all the distress and shots. It is a wonder that he escaped alive."

Another said: "They all did well. They held their ground lying or standing, and they charged and took their death wounds like brave men."

The Schleswiger shook his head and brought his hand down heavily on his knee. "To think that that could have happened to us!" he said.

They mentioned two more good names of old Africans who had led and fallen.

I spoke up now in a loud voice: "There is a remarkably large number of dead and few wounded"; but Hansen said: "Don't be so stupid. They don't make prisoners. We don't, either." Then they said again that we should most likely have a battle now, and, if we did, it would be a very severe one.

While I was still sitting with them and listening, balls of red and white fire were shot as signals out of great pistols, from the middle of our camp up straight into the evening sky. Many of us stood up on the wagons and on branches of trees and watched out over the vast, dark, silent bush to see if an answer came from the main division. But no answer came.

When quiet was commanded in camp, I went back to my division. Our corporal had not come back. The next day I was promoted to be corporal. The buttons which Gehlsen gave me I sewed on with white thread. There was no black to be had.

We remained several days more in this place. Several scouting parties went and came every day; but none of them saw anything of the enemy. And still no messenger or signals came from the main division. We talked a great deal about our situation, and thought the enemy, forced to the east by the main army, would someday come upon us with their thousands, and would run over us in order to break through into the wilderness. That might well be a hard position for us.

After a few days, the water got scarce and bad; so, we broke camp one afternoon and marched with great caution, for it was to be expected that the enemy, who on account of their numerous herds of cattle needed a great deal of water and had possession of the next waterholes, said to be very plenteous ones, would defend them zealously.

Some sections had to make sallies on both sides, slinking crouched down among the bushes, with their guns ready in their hands. I was ordered to this work.

As our main body advanced swiftly on the unimpeded way, we who had to be always ahead of them at one side were obliged to run, slink, duck, leap, and keep continually on the alert. This went on for seven hours. When I was relieved, I was dead tired. The soles of my boots, which had been torn for two weeks already, were loose and my feet were sore. Before we went on again, I tied up my soles with thongs of fresh ox-skin and pulled great thorns out of my hands and arms.

We marched well into the night, which was particularly dark. In the middle of the night the command came suddenly from the head of the column to halt and push up together. The wagons came up together in haste, and we knelt in a square around them, facing out with our guns ready. We thought the attack was coming now. We were all eager for it. But it didn't come and soon the command was given: "Stack arms, and take blankets." We stationed guards and camped there for the night.

Early the next day we went on unhindered and reached the water place about noon. It was a rather large field, white from the limy soil. In several deep holes, there was quite a good deal of good water. There we camped.

Next morning our company set out to find the place where the big scouting party had fought and been half annihilated. After a long, difficult march through thick bush and past several shallow ponds containing good water, we saw, toward noon, numberless eagles and vultures perching on trees, or hovering in the air over the brush-field. We went toward them and came to a cleared space, which at one end ran up a little slope where the brush was growing again and where, already partially concealed by the new growth, stood some huts of the enemy. On this slope, in the long, dry grass in front of the huts, lay the naked, mutilated, half-devoured bodies of many of our men. Some of us were silent; some gnashed their teeth, doubled up their fists, and cursed; others mocked and said: "How long will it be before we are lying that way? Then we shall have no more suffering."

We placed men on guard in the bush about us and began to search for the other dead, especially those who had made an attack into the bush and had fallen there, and we found them all. Then some dug graves, others wove wreaths of the dry grass, others made crosses of pieces of wood, and still others cut the thorn bushes, which were hard as horn, with knives or side-arms. Then we laid the dead in their graves, shovelled the earth over them, laid the thorny branches we had cut as a barrier over the place so that the wild animals and men would leave them in peace, and returned again to the camp.

CHAPTER 8

A Memorable Easter

This evening or the next morning a reconnoitring party came back with the news that it looked as if the enemy intended to break through toward the east at the south of us. As this movement would threaten our provision line, and as, moreover, no news had yet come from the main division, and without it our small number could hardly withstand the onslaught of thousands, the major decided to go back about three days' march to our old water place and to lie in wait in a fortified camp until news should come.

So, we started on the return journey. We were all depressed; many were weary and dull. When we came, after some hours' marching, to a beautiful great forest with trees which looked like German oaks, we were strongly reminded of our native land, and we became a little brighter and more lively while passing through it. We crossed the dry, sandy bed of a river, which lay a yard deeper than its banks, and then on again through quite narrow bush paths.

While we were encamped that night, we at last saw signals to the south west of us. They flashed out five or six times in red or white rockets and aroused and excited us. We thought they were signals from the main division, and that now we should start out and charge the enemy. Weeks afterward we learned that it was the enemy, who, finding some rockets near our dead, had shot them off for sport. We were quieter than usual this evening. It was the night before Easter.

This evening Behrens bequeathed to me, in case he fell, his pistols, which he had brought with him from Kiel; and I bequeathed him my watch and chain, which I had earned by voluntarily helping in the workshop when I was a fourteen-year-old boy. Otto Hargens, a one-year volunteer from Ditmarsh, a bright young fellow who was promoted to be under officer that evening, was witness.

51

The next morning, while it was still dark, we made a fine Easter fire of dried thorn-bush in the middle of the camp, and all stood about it and gazed into it and were glad that we were still alive, although our life was so dirty and friendless and painful; and we thought of home, picturing how the mother was giving out the Sunday clothes, and how clean the living-room was, and how festive the morning coffee, and how the church-bells were ringing out over the houses.

Just at this hour, in the grey of the morning, a great company of the enemy was really moving to the east, not in order to break through into the wilderness, but in order to lie in wait for us in an especially bushy part of the road we should pass that day.

About six o'clock, when the Easter sun had risen bright and clear, we broke camp. We proceeded in the following order: first, the little group of cavalry which still remained to us, on their emaciated, wounded, and rough-coated horses; then a company marching; then our cannon; then our fifty wagons, each with a team of twenty-four oxen; and then my company. I went in the first platoon. Behind this, as the rear of the whole column, at a distance of about three hundred yards, marched a half-platoon. The whole column was about two miles and a half long. On the narrow, dusty road, which wound in many curves through the thick bush, only a small part of it could be seen at a time. But one heard from the cracking of whips and the shouting of the negro drivers, "*Wörk, Wörk, Osse!*" how the procession was going forward.

I was passing, in my thoughts of home, through our whole house. I went to the door and looked down the street where the people were going to church, and I turned back into the kitchen where mother was inspecting my little sisters to see if they were properly dressed for going to church. How peaceful and clean and lovely it all was there! And I was really here and tired, hungry, clad in dirty rags, marching through a foreign land, far, far away from my home, in the midst of a wild, heathen enemy. So, I mused, and I believe I heard the Easter bells as they pealed slowly and waveringly out over the city.

Then two bullets fell not far behind me. I woke up, and I thought at first that an officer had gone into the bush and fired at some game.

We went on, but the next moment—while now shot followed upon shot behind us, and we turned around with our guns ready to fire—a man came by breathless, running to the front and calling: "The rear is under fire!" The officers immediately ordered us to press forward into the bushes. I was already running with Behrens and Gehlsen into the bush and then toward the shots in the direction from which we had come. I had pressed forward a little way when I saw two clouds of smoke rising among bushes in front of me. I hastily raised my gun to my cheek and fired standing.

At that same moment, I saw something at my side fall heavily, as a log falls. When I had fired, I saw that Behrens was lying there in convulsions. I sprang diagonally forward behind the next bush, with others following, dropped on one knee, and delivered a furious, rapid fire in the direction of the smoke at some dark thing which was moving behind the bush. I don't know how many times I fired. Then my other comrade, who was kneeling beside me, fell, and in falling dropped his gun. He groaned aloud. I threw myself down and fired quickly in order, as had been previously arranged, to call the attention of other comrades to where I lay hard pressed. They sprang up, threw themselves down at intervals and shot as I was doing at an enemy of whom we saw nothing but little clouds of smoke here and there among the bushes.

We were lying like logs. Close by me was an under officer whose left arm was bleeding badly. He had propped his gun on a dry branch and was firing at short regular intervals. Bullets were coming from in front and both sides. Now I saw something strange coming at us. In a mass, it lay and kneeled and slipped through the bushes. I saw no single individual, only a group. It came quite near, and the balls splintered the bush around me. I shouted as loud as I could: "Here, this way!" I almost think that we could have held our own in that place till re-enforcements had arrived, but just then came the command from the captain, "Keep low and fall back!"

I sprang up with four companions and ran back one or two bushes and flung myself down again. Three of us reached there; one, who was hit as he was leaping, stumbled and fell. He tried to creep after us, moaning piteously. I lay and shot over him and moved a little to one side because he was raising his arms in agony. Again, we sprang up, and while on the run, the man next me clutched at his breast, let his gun fall, leaned sideways against a bush, and while still standing said, with a look at me: "Give my brother the book." Then he fell heavily and did not stir again.

I could not search for the book, for at that moment as I turned to shoot, I saw here and there in the grey-green bushes, strange men in cord uniform rising like snakes out of the grass. Glancing around me, I saw that I was alone. Then I sprang up and in three or four leaps joined some other soldiers, who were now going forward stooping, and turned and knelt among them to shoot. I saw not far from me a black, half-naked figure like an ape, holding his gun in his mouth, and climbing with hands and feet into a tree. I aimed at him and screamed aloud for joy when he fell down the trunk.

When I wanted to fire again and was bending my forefinger, my hand suddenly became powerless. I got very angry and looked at it in a rage. Then I saw blood running out of my ragged sleeve and I felt that my arm from the elbow down was wet. I heard a dull, wild screaming and calling of the enemy in a half-circle around me. There was no one near me anymore. I recalled then the words which my father had so often said to me, "When you stick your nose into anything, you forget everything else." I crept hastily back for a little distance on all fours, and then springing up, ran on in a crouching position.

There was still one man running near me, all hanging over to one side, with his body bleeding. I seized him under the arm as we ran, but he fell groaning on one knee and bent together as he knelt. I took his gun so that it might not fall into the hands of the enemy. My own I had thrown over my shoulder. I ran on in this way and came, with my comrades, who were pressing forward, into a clearing.

There I saw the old major standing straight and placid in the middle of the place, with some officers and men about him. Sections kept breaking through from the other side of the road and dispersed themselves at a motion of his hand round about him in the clearing, and throwing themselves upon the ground fired at the enemy. Behind the men who had come up running came the cannon in all haste; in obedience to his motion they were turned about just in front of him and were fired over the companies lying in front, into the enemy.

Near a revolving cannon both my guns fell from my grasp, my knees lost their strength, and I collapsed. I looked in despair at my bloody arm. While I was cowering there, I reached for the roll of bandage that I had in my coat and I managed to get it; but when I wanted to tie it around my arm, the blood would not stop and a sailor helped me. Some wounded men were already lying and kneeling there, and others with faces drawn with pain came creeping up and lay down behind the cannon, which were firing steadily.

Soon after, when the ammunition wagons and ambulances came galloping up, I stood up and tried to pull along a chest of ammunition which had been knocked open with axes. I could help only for a while, I don't know how long, for suddenly my knees, which I had held firm by main force, gave way under me. I slunk back again to the other wounded men and sat with them, stemming with my left hand the blood which was pouring from my wounded arm. Sometimes I would look up; and when I did, I always saw the old major searching the whole clearing with his eyes.

The other men stood or lay in a half-circle around the wounded and the sick—who had been removed from the wagons and were lying indifferent with flushed faces under their blankets—and fired furiously at the enemy, who were pressing up close. They came so near that I saw them. Most of them wore the uniform of our home guards; but some had European summer suits on and some were half naked. Their limbs seemed remarkably long, their motions remarkably smooth and tortuous. They slipped and glided and leaped through the bush toward us. Two or three times the artillery fired with shrapnel. It roared through the air like a cataract; than it rattled and crackled, and the enemy gave way. In this way our men, lying and standing about us, held out for two hours against a wild onslaught, but were unable to advance a step.

Finally, however, they began to press forward in the bush, forced back the enemy, and pushed their way to the place where we, the rear company, had fought, hoping probably to find some who still lived; but they were all dead and stripped. They brought in the bodies and laid them in a semicircle under a tree. I, with some others, started toward them; I wanted to see my two dearest comrades once more, but we were hurried back that we might not see the pitiable sight. Some comrades were already digging a grave; others were barricading the camp, for we were to spend the night here.

Toward evening, as the sun was setting, the dead were laid in the ground; twenty men fired over their open grave; the old major talked of the Fatherland and God, and of death and the Easter faith. I sat sore and half beside myself, leaning against the side of a wagon by the wounded, some of whom were talking softly, others sighing painfully, others sleeping from exhaustion or lying in a stupor, and one or two already gasping in death. Gehlsen, who also had a flesh wound in his arm, sat near me, and they brought us some rice and a cook-pan cover full of water, about a pint. I would gladly have drunk three quarts, but far or near there was no water. I felt very forlorn and suffered torturing homesickness.

It was lucky for me that Hansen and Wilkins came and, taking hold of me under the arms, carried me over to their companions, the old

Africans, and gave me secretly more water and a piece of dry pancake and a blanket. They were always somewhat better provided than we were. I sat there and heard with dulled senses what they were saying. They said that the fight had been a slight victory, for the enemy had fled; but it was a success too dearly bought. They said, also, that they had not given the enemy credit for such great bravery, and thought it probable that they would attack us again in the morning.

I also heard them talk of our sick men; they said that with such miserable fare and foul water many more would be sick. I wondered in my half-sleep why they made so much account of the sick ones and did not talk much more of the two and thirty who lay in the ground under the big tree, and of their parents and brothers and sisters. I had grown more and more weary, and had wrapped myself in my blanket and had laid my burning arm on my hip, and heard only now and then a word, till all around me seemed quiet. Then there began again to be a movement in the bushes. In my troubled sleep, I heard shots again and saw black men round about me, climbing trees, their guns in their mouths. The old Africans stood on all sides of me and hit with every shot; but there were too many of the enemy and one came and seized me by the arm and wanted to take away my protecting blanket. Then I groaned, and half awake, half asleep, heard Henry Hansen say: "Let him lie there. I don't need a blanket. I have the hide of an elephant."

The next morning, we had a little rice and water. Then the sick and wounded, two of whom were unconscious, were lifted into wagons. I seated myself on the chest in the front of the wagon, my arm, which stung and burned, in a sling. Behind me, in the long, covered wagon, in two rows, lay four wounded and two sick men. The negro by the oxen raised his long thin arms for the first swing of the whip and shouted to the beasts. Then the wagon wheel struck against the first stone which lay in the rut and fell down off it, jolting heavily, and behind me I heard painful groans. I was supporting my well arm on my knee. We went on in a long, long train, wagon after wagon, with cannon, and comrades marching, scattered in between.

As we passed the great grave under the tree, every one cast once more a long look upon it. Those that forgot it at first turned and looked back. I thought as I passed:

"If God brings me back to my home, and gives me health and a long life, I will stand before that grave once more and think whether I am worthy in my own eyes to have come alive out of that den of fire."

Then the dead lay alone.

One fellow, the one who had a shot in the body, was being tortured slowly to death by his wound. In the morning, he still spoke short words in a low voice; at noon, he took a little of the dirty water; soon after you could hear the heavy rattling in his throat, and later he became unconscious. Toward evening he lay with open mouth and set eyes, but I noticed from the rising and sinking of his dirty woollen blanket that he still lived. One of our one-year volunteers, a surgeon, came at every stop and looked into the wagon, and I saw quick sympathy in his eyes. He was not much older than I, but he had grown a long, heavy beard in the bush.

When at nightfall I waked from a half-sleep, a man from the first platoon, a Rhinelander, was sitting near me on the chest. He complained of weakness in his feet and knees, and felt first hot and then cold. He looked at me out of deep, dry eyes in a strangely confused way, and great drops of sweat came out on his forehead. The surgeon came, felt his pulse, looked suspiciously at him, saying to himself, "That is the twelfth in seven days," and went away again.

At evening, we reached our old camp, where we were to remain on our guard against the enemy and wait for news.

CHAPTER 9

Destitution and Misery

That night I couldn't sleep on account of fever. I lay with open eyes near the hospital and watched them caring for the sick and wounded. They took a tent canvas, folded it once, stuffed long, dry grass into the sack thus formed, laid the sufferers upon it, and did all they could for their comfort. Toward morning a new patient came in; he walked with dragging feet and half-closed eyes, pale as death. In the forenoon two more came. There were already about seventeen wounded and fourteen sick lying there. The sick ones lay as apathetic as if they had been stunned by a blow on the head. If anyone questioned them, they said they felt no pain, but were exhausted and hot. In the next three days twelve more were sick. So, it went from day to day. It began to be said openly that it was typhoid fever due to the insufficient, poor food and foul water, and to the filth and chilling in the thin, ragged clothing.

When in the morning we had brewed our coffee at as big a fire as we could make so as to warm ourselves after the cold night, our comrades would come up and practice grips as if they were in the barrack-yard at Kiel. Then they swarmed in squads into the bush, crept and slunk and ducked, threw themselves and lay ready for an attack, aimed against the sun and with the sun, and sprang up and stormed with "Hurrah!" But the old Africans jeered and said they weren't shouting "Hurrah!" but "Hunger."

At twelve the voice of the sergeant sounded from the wagons, "Get rations." The men to whom that duty was intrusted ran up and came back under the canvas with a little flour and rice and salt and unroasted coffee. Then in every mess there began fire-making and stirring and talking and advice and spooning and eating. I couldn't do anything more than carry a little water. At three, drill began again. The men sat in the rifle-pits in squads under corporals and cleaned their arms. I sat with them. Conversation was slow and dragging. A melancholy song was started: "*Zu Strassburg auf der Schanz'*," or "*Steh' ich in finstrer Mitternacht.*" But it sounded dull and soon died out.

It got dark very quickly evenings. We used to sit in the lee of a tent canvas and talk of all sorts of things and sing songs. From the tent of the old major we would catch the sound of a laugh or an invective. Out of the dark opening of the long hospital tent flashed the wandering light of the orderly as he went from one to another. Here and there a light would glimmer in a fire-hole. Under the trees the negroes used to sit and sing in unison a choral taught them by the missionaries. Then an officer off duty would come by from the non-commissioned officers' posts which surrounded the camp, and calling shortly to the negroes to hold their tongues, "Will jelle slap,'" would go into his tent.

So, passed one day like another. Wonderful rumours flew continually through the camp: a thousand cavalry were on the way from Germany to help us; the governor had beaten the negroes in a battle lasting two days; there were numberless negroes killed and their bodies had been burned on pyres. Probably the conversation turned no less than fifty times upon the subject of our dismissal and return home. That was our favourite theme! Home! What happy faces they would wear there! What shouldn't we have to tell? When the little reconnoitring party of five or six men on thin, worn-out horses came back it was soon known at every cooking-hole what they had reported, and we founded great assertions on the news. Each one was a staff-officer and wiser than all the rest. And then when we have beaten the enemy one way or another we'll go home! That was always the conclusion. Oh, to go home! We all, every one of us, wanted to go home.

The oppressive heat of the days and the piercing cold of the nights, the wretched fare and the miserable water, were making more and more of the men weak, sluggish, and indifferent. We all spoke another language, without life and without emphasis, just as though we were drunk with sleep. Some few kept cheerful. Henry Gehlsen used often to come and cheer me up. In spite of his wounded arm he was always active and interested in everything new that he saw: in a bird in the air, in a cloud in the sky, in the speech of the black drivers, and in the fever of the sick ones. Henry Hansen, the old guardsman, used to nod surreptitiously to me, and in the shelter of the commissariat wagon would slip a morsel of cold pancake into my hand. My arm, which had been shot through, was feverish and painful, and besides that I had a horrid oppressed feeling in my body, and I was so exhausted that sometimes in broad daylight, as I sat at the fire-hole and watched the life about me, my eyes would shut, my chin would drop on my breast, and I would slowly fall over to one side and sleep.

Singing in camp was now becoming more and more infrequent and conversation more and more forced. We were getting continually dirtier, hungrier, and sicker. Apathetic and silent, we saw every night one or two of our number laid in the strange, grey earth, clad in their torn, dirty rags and wrapped in their grey woollen blankets. Heavily and wearily those who were commanded to shoot in honour of the dead raised their arms; wearily and with dulled senses they shovelled the earth over their comrades and laid thorn branches above them. In the night, I used to be wakened by the tired, delirious talking of the sick ones, and by the howling of the jackals which scented the graves.

After we had been for two weeks in this camp, matters had come to such a pass that every fourth man was sick. They lay in full uniform in two long rows on the ground, with tent canvas stretched over them as protection from the burning sun. They had to lie there, seriously sick, not only without any sort of medicine, but also without proper nourishment. We had neither milk nor eggs. We hadn't even a piece of dry bread. We hadn't even a bit of cleanliness.

The old major conducted himself as though he had good courage still, and did everything he could think of for us. The last joy on earth to many a one was a kind, cheerful word spoken by him. I used often to see him coming out of the hospital tent and often was gladdened by his kindly consolation. But when more and more of us fell ill, and more and more went indifferently about their work, and still no news or provisions or hospital supplies came, even he had to give up hope. He probably thought of going on again, but he realised that his little troop would no longer present the appearance of an army, but rather that of a transport of sick soldiers. Then he sent messengers to the main division to report that he was powerless and must desist from harassing the enemy, and that he could not any longer see this dying off of the young men, and that he wanted to seek a place with a better water-supply.

Then they packed those who were severely wounded and the sick on the wagons, while I crouched inactive, with dull, confused head, and inflamed and burning arm, by the wheel of the ammunition wagon.

The well men marched beside and behind the wagon. A few sat on worn, rough horses. So, we started on a depressing journey. I sat in the provision wagon conducted by Hansen. We used to sit side by side for hours while he smoked his short pipe and spoke an occasional word.

Once a man in delirium sprang right out of the wagon into the bush and was never seen again. Then guards had to be stationed about the wagons so that no one could escape. One of those who had the fever attacked a doctor with his side-arms, and another who was still in the ranks shot wildly around him. Three of the sick died on the way and were buried in the bush. The one-year volunteer was surgeon, nurse, and soldier, all in one. His face was growing narrower and paler, but his beard was getting longer and thicker.

On the third night, several oxen collapsed and one died. We stopped our wagon to help them. I don't know how it happened that the rest of the force went on. They probably thought that the place for bivouac was close by and that we would follow immediately. But we were delayed an hour. Then we continued on the narrow road in the bush, in the dark night,—ten sick men with three men to protect them and the drivers saying they had seen the enemy in the bush. I climbed painfully into the wagon and told the two wounded men, who were partly in possession of their senses and had some strength, how things stood with us. They half sat up and took their guns and held watch with us till we could go on.

On the fourth day of our retreat we reached a good water-supply. There was there a small, very simple church which the mission had built, and the partially destroyed house of the missionary. In this building beds made of grass and blankets were prepared on the ground. The well men encamped some hundred yards above on a hill. There we were to remain until the disease had run itself out among us. At that time, we heard that the campaign had come to a standstill for the present, because the insurrection had assumed too great proportions for the small German force which was at the time available in the colony.

When we had been encamped there for about ten days, provisions finally arrived, and mattresses and also strengthening food for the sick; such things as wine, bouillon, white of egg, cocoa, and Quaker oats, so that at last they had beds and enough to eat. We, too, were well fed, but we still had to go on wearing our horribly dirty clothing.

We lived in the greatest despondency, all sick, and some dying every day. I made myself useful as far as I could. Languid and with dull head, I went about among the sick; with my sound left hand gave water to one and a piece of *zwieback* to another, and helped a third to sit up a little to attend to the needs of nature.

In these miserable, gloomy weeks two comrades came especially near to me. Formerly, when we were well, we had hardly known one another. One was a Thuringian boy, with childlike, brown eyes, who said little. Even on the ship it had struck me that he was very silent and looked surprised at everything. Afterwards, when we had landed and pushed our way into the bush, his eyes became more and more timid, and his mouth more and more mutely closed. For the rest, he had a strong body and bore everything well and without complaining, and he stood his ground in a fight.

Now he was sick in bed. With his gun and his blanket, he had come down to us from the camp, shivering and with dull eyes, and he said, with a shy attempt at a jest, as he lay down: "Now I shall be a gentleman of leisure with you the rest of my days." I now talked often with him, more by signs and suggestion than by means of words, for our throats were dried-out tubes and our thoughts had dragging feet. Then I understood that to him everything which we had experienced since leaving Kiel had been uncanny and horrible,—the everlasting expanse of the open sea, the forbidding, defiant coast of England, the sublime Peak of Teneriffe, the unfamiliar constellations, the scorching sun, the bare shore of Swakopmund, the sight of our dead, the dying of comrades. For all these great and hard things, his soul was not tough enough. He died of dysentery and heart weakness on the seventh day.

The other was already very sick when we moved into this camp. He was born in Nuremberg and had spent his childhood there. When he was fifteen years old he had left his home because of a stepfather, and since that time had wandered restlessly over the world. He had travelled out to South America from Bremen as a steward, had gone straight through to Chile, had seen Samoa, and had been a waiter in San Francisco. There he had enlisted in the United States Navy, but not for long. A few hundred *marks* in his pocket had enabled him to travel from New Orleans to Australia to dig gold, but he found little or none. When Australia was enlisting volunteers to fight against the Boers, he had come over as a trimmer, but to help the Boers. He was captured and had survived some bad days on the Island of Ceylon. From there he had returned to Cape Town, and, at the first news of revolt in our colony, had volunteered. I believe there are not many Germans who wander so restlessly and madly and with such foolish good-nature through the world.

The whole life of such is passed running indiscriminately, at the first impulse of a restless, unstable mind, into the right or wrong path, and after that course is run, plunging without reflection or regret at the next object which comes just then into their field of vision. He railed against the English, the Americans, and most of all against the Boers, but I was convinced that he would have run to the Japanese or the French if there had been any trouble in those quarters.

It is bad when a human being has no control over his life. He was lying now very sick with typhoid fever, indulging in all sorts of fancies, although he had so confidently believed and boasted that he was too well hardened to be sick. When he was slowly recovering he became perfectly reasonable and narrated to me his whole life. For an entire week, however, he clung to the delusion that both his legs had been shot off. Many an hour I sat by him, and I learned a great deal from his conversation. What became of him afterwards I do not know.

I was still strong enough to keep about on my feet, but once when I went out of camp, as I was obliged to do many times a day, I found that I had symptoms of dysentery. Then I went back to the others, all my courage gone, and I sat and brooded and firmly believed that I should have to die here; and I reconciled myself to this fate with mournful reflections and thought sadly of my parents. I said nothing to the surgeon, but there was a hospital attendant there whom I asked about it and he said: "You have typhoid in one part of your body and dysentery in another, but you have a lucky nature and you'll pull through." And he gave me some pills.

I took the pills exactly as he directed; but I didn't believe the rest of his preaching, for he was half out of his mind. There were many in this campaign, officers, surgeons, hospital attendants, and soldiers, who were still doing their duty faithfully, just as an engine continues to run for a little while after the steam is shut off; but inwardly they were already sick and full of confused visions. One evening—I had already been for weeks in the typhoid hospital—someone had received a letter, I think from Swakopmund. In it among other things it was said that everybody in Germany was talking about the Russo-Japanese war, but nobody mentioned us; indeed, people made sport of us and our distress as they do of men who are contending for a ridiculous and lost cause, and they didn't want to hear anything about us because they said we didn't understand how to make a quick conquest.

I wanted at first to throw away the letter, but then I thought I would show it to Henry Hansen. He didn't come, however, but the next day another old guardsman came and I showed him the letter, for all my courage had deserted me.

He read it and laughed, saying:

What surprises you in that? Hasn't it always been so? How many wives has the King of Siam? What kind of garters does the Queen of Spain wear? What answer did you get to the postcard you sent the Japanese general? See! That's the sort of thing that interests the German. You just ought to hear how the English on every street-corner laugh at us Johnnies and boasters. The Englishman asks at every turn of affairs: 'What use will this be to me and to England?'

And with that he went off.

I went back to my sick comrades, fetched my blanket, and seated myself on the ground at one side of the entrance to the hospital tent. It was a cold, disagreeable evening. In the thicket, dry branches were snapping; vultures were flying toward the high trees which rose thick and dark above the bush.

From behind me came intermittently the loud wailing of a very sick soldier. A fellow who was slightly sick sat crouched down in front of the provision tent on a chest that had been half smashed in and sang in a melancholy, weary voice, our old song:—

Dooh mein Schicksal will es nimmer,
Durch die Welt ich wandern mass.
Trantes Heim, dein denk' ich immer,
Trantes Heim, dir gilt mein Gross.
 Sei gegriisflt in weiter Ferae,
Teure Heimat, sei gegrtisst.

Two comrades, wrapped in their cloaks, their spades on their shoulders, went across to the hill, to dig a new grave.

CHAPTER 11

Civilization and a Bath

In the fourth week of my stay in the typhoid camp I heard that fresh troops had come from Germany and that still more would come, all hussars, four thousand in all, and that now the campaign was to go forward with more vigour. But to me that was all indifferent news, and I thought: "If you were only out of this monkey-land!"

But in the fifth week the force of my disease was spent. As health and strength slowly returned, I thought that it wasn't good to go home after such experiences as I had had. I wanted to be on hand for the second and better part of the campaign, for the "quick conquest."

It happened that a first lieutenant with a little scouting party of three men came to us from the east. On the way, he had lost one man, and he had to leave another as a typhoid patient. One day I stopped him and begged him to take me with him. He asked me if I could ride.

I said, "Yes," although I had not sat on a horse since the days of my childhood, and even then never on a saddle.

He looked at me distrustfully and said: "You'll fall off your horse on the way."

"At your service, sir," I said, "I am as strong as a tree"; and I looked at him. He was thin as a rail, and his eyes glittered under his forehead.

"I have led a dog's life for four months," said he.

"At your service, sir," I said, "so have I, and for that reason I want to get away from here."

Then he got my dismissal from the captain.

Before morning dawned, I went to the horses, which were already standing tied to our wagons, and said to the under officer, who was one of the party and was standing near the horses, that I had never yet ridden on a saddle. He abused me roundly at first and asked me if

I knew even which end of a horse was the front and which the back. I thought to myself, "Don't make him quite wild," and I seized the saddle, went up to the animal, and recalling to mind how I had in my life seen a horse saddled, put it on not so far wrong. Then he began again to berate me violently and to show me how to do it right. Then I practiced mounting and dismounting and thought: "That will do, all right."

The next day I learned from the other man that the under-officer had only a little while before mounted a horse for the first time in his life, and had made a great deal more fuss about it than I. Then I wondered at the extraordinary boarders on God's earth. Indeed, I have often been amazed at them.

So, on that morning, after I had been four months in the bush and wilderness, I rode with the scouting party to the west, to Windhuk. My companions had been out here just as long as I. I was very much in fear of the first trot, but it went tolerably well. With light heart but sore body I rode along, energetically nodding my head all the time. The next day it went much better. The lieutenant, a tall Rhinelander, was a pleasant man; he often talked with me and seemed pleased with me.

After we had ridden for two days through a barren, deserted region, we began to approach the city. When we saw from afar the first telegraph pole, we called one another's attention to it, and we surveyed the long, thin thing with joyous eyes. As we rode by the first house that wasn't roofless and hadn't burned-out window-holes, we admired it very much, and when we noticed that proper furniture, a table and chairs, were standing on the open veranda, we stared in astonishment and turned in our saddles to look till we had passed.

With wide-open eyes, we gazed into the garden, which in former years the colonist had laid out with great care. There were really the palms and arbours of which we had dreamed and talked in Kiel and on the water, and there was a pond! Oh, if only we could ride into it! And there in the shade of the veranda stood a German woman, and she held a little child on her arm. How we looked! How we rejoiced over the light clean dress she wore, and her friendly face, and the little white child! We gazed as though at a miracle from heaven at a sight any one could see every day in Germany,—just like the three holy kings who came out of the desert and looked from their horses upon Mary and her child. She looked at us, ragged, dirty, hungry fellows, and bowed in a friendly way, with big sympathetic eyes, when we all, as though at a command, raised our hands to our caps.

Weary, but with spirit, our horses mounted the sandy road to the fort. In the yard, where there were some soldiers and some Hottentot women, we dismounted and looked after our horses. The lieutenant went to the commandant to make his report.

But I, when we had cared for our beasts, walked across the yard, stretching my arms out on both sides—so disgusting did I seem to myself—and went into a room and had given out to me a whole, new cord uniform, with riding boots. I pushed back my ragged left sleeve and laid the clothes over my arm and went in a hurry straight over to the bathhouse, where I tore off my rags, plunged into the water, and washed and soaped and scrubbed till my whole body was red.

When I came out into the yard again in my fine new home-guard uniform, the lieutenant was talking with a citizen and did not recognise me. Then he laughed and said something to the man about me, at which the latter turned and said: "I am the husband of the woman who was standing with her child on the veranda when you rode by. She would like to thank you for your friendly greeting. Will you be our guest this evening?" I was so pleased that I blushed.

So that evening, after I had had another bath and had scrubbed myself again, I went out to the neighbourhood of the house and waited till the lieutenant had gone in and then went in just behind him. When I entered the living-room the man shook hands with me, and his wife talked kindly to me and showed me the child; and then I sat down with them at the table and stared dumbly at the white table-cloth and the plates and the bread and milk and sugar; and I listened to the woman's lovely voice. In that hour, I could have been overhappy if I had been able to keep from thinking of my sick and dead comrades.

When I took my leave after supper and went up to the fort, I saw some soldiers laughing with Hottentot women, and one fellow said to me as he passed that these women were at our disposal at any time. That made me angry, and I went up to the long veranda that lies to the west. I stood there a long time and looked over to the mountains, gilded by the sinking sun; and I thought of home with violent longing.

I lived for three weeks at the fort, and from the better food that I received there, and from the cleanliness which I enjoyed, I regained strength more and more. I wrote three whole days on a detailed letter home, and I often went to the house of the merchant to play with the baby and to talk with its parents.

As the campaign at this time had come entirely to a standstill, the enemy were very bold. Their mounted parties came down from the north and harassed and surprised our commissariat trains, our scouting parties, and our cattle guards. They even dared to come close to the capital, and drove off our cattle and shot several of our men. I often sat on horseback with others to watch for them, but we seldom got a shot at them.

I had a great deal of conversation with fellow-soldiers who were in this command, or who, like myself, were at Windhuk on account of illness, or who came and went; and with the Boers whom the government had taken on as freight-carriers, and with farmers who had fled here from the bush.

Among all these various men who had gathered here from all quarters, and were always coming and going, the wildest rumours were rife. For though in war times especially distorted reports are always coming to light anew and are believed and spread abroad by excited minds, South Africa in particular, from Congo to the Cape, on account of its incipient and rapidly and restlessly developing political life, and on account of the immense distances, and the numberless idle hours which trekking with oxen causes, was spun over with a monstrous gossip. One may say that South Africa is like a great building in process of construction, in all the rooms of which mechanics are pounding and hammering. The noise resounds loud and clear through all the great, empty rooms.

But often after such talks I used to go out alone on the veranda and look off into the broad country to the west and see the sun set. And as it sank, I saw light, white clouds descend out of the sky and spread out like a garment. And I watched the garment sink slowly down before the sun to the earth, and I saw how the departing sun painted it all the colours of the rainbow. Blended in delicate stripes, they glided down to the earth. At the side to the south shone a mighty mountain range of naked stone, which reflected the light like metal; but in the parts where the failing light no longer reached it, it menaced hard and gloomy. I stood watching it with ever new wonder until the whole beautiful picture faded and night and the stars came quickly on. And the stars were beautiful, too! How wonderfully hot they glowed in the deep black sky! But I only thought, at the sight of all this splendour of the day and night:

"Oh, Africa, if I were only at home!"

CHAPTER 12

Another Expedition

At the beginning of the fourth week I felt that I had entirely re-gained my health, and the lazy life here was becoming loathsome to me. Just in this week the lieutenant was preparing himself to go north to the front; so, I told him what I had at heart, that I would gladly go on and make the new campaign with him. He started up as he usually did, and grumbled: "What! you want to go with me? Where are the others, then?"

I replied: "One third are dead; another third are sick and wounded; the rest are scattered here and there in military posts."

He regarded me thoughtfully and said: "You poor rascals! You were so smart and saucy when you arrived and you have experienced noth-ing but suffering and death. Haven't you had enough of it? Well, I'll take you down with me." I was very glad and bought for myself all sorts of trifles, and on the third day we set out.

After a day's journey toward the coast we reached a great station where all the necessaries which had come from the coast for the new campaign were stored: horses from Argentine; oxen and wagons from Cape Town; horses, ammunition, clothing, preserves, and hospital sup-plies from Germany. When I had passed through this place five months before, it had consisted of five or six houses of corrugated iron; now it was an army encampment. In the station building, where the general and his staff were, officers, orderlies, and dispatch messengers, most of whom, not having been in the bush, were pretty clean, were running in and out. A crowd of young officers and privates were breaking a lot of horses and mules, only just come from Argentine, to harness or saddle.

I have never in my life heard a man storm and swear as did one lieutenant who, with twenty men all in shirtsleeves, with long ropes in their hands, was working among a lot of mules which were almost as excited as the men themselves. Batteries were standing in the ranks being cleaned, tried, and harnessed up. In front of some long tents, in which enormous quantities of food stores were piled, were great covered wagons, getting their loads. Black drivers were coming from the distant meadow, screaming loudly at the oxen which they harnessed, twelve pair to each wagon.

The Boer, proprietor of wagon, oxen, and drivers, seated himself on the brilliantly painted chest which stood in the front of the wagon, or himself took the long whip. Then the escort came up. With loud geeing and hawing the procession started northward out of the camp, in a cloud of dust. From the wheelwright and blacksmith shop were heard pounding and ringing of metal until late in the night. From the canteens came loud laughter and talk.

From the front, on the north, open columns were coming in daily, most of them bringing along sick men. As I came up to one wagon which had just arrived, the surgeon had already climbed in and was talking to a sick fellow: "Well, my boy, how goes it? Oh, answer! You can just tell me how you are, can't you?" Then he turned to the man lying next and said: "Why doesn't he say anything?"

The man spoken to gathered himself together out of his confusion and said in Low German: "He's dead."

The surgeon turned to the guards and said: "Why didn't you bury him on the way?"

They replied: "We didn't want to leave him there alone; we hadn't time to bury him properly, and the jackals would have dug him out again."

Beside the dead on the hard boards of the wagon lay the living, most of them unconscious or out of their heads, wearing their uniforms and boots, with their guns and soft hats beside them, their lips and tongues parched, and their eye-sockets deep and blue. In this condition, they had been on the road for a week.

The hospital was a long barrack of corrugated iron. I heard that an acquaintance from Itzehoe was lying there, and I went in to visit him. Row upon row of typhoid patients lay close together, each one with a mosquito net stretched around him, like a baby in its carriage. Some lay silent, with pale, sunken eyes; others cheered on the horses in loud tones, or saw fire-light, or shouted commands, each in the dialect of his province, Low-German, Saxon, or Bavarian; others were convalescent and lay there pale, following me with their eyes. One nodded to me. The man from Itzehoe was unconscious. When I was again outside, I drew a deep breath; and I was depressed for a long time. There was a flag on the hospital which the officer on guard used to raise every morning, but it was no use; every forenoon an orderly would make a short report to him and the flag would be hauled down.

On the fourth day, we set out with a commissariat train of six Cape wagons, with Boers, drivers, and oxen, which was conducted by the first lieutenant. Ten men, all mounted, escorted the train as guard. I was responsible for three wagons, and rode a dark brown Argentine horse, which, though thin, was in good condition.

Just as we, amid cracking of whips and great hallooing on the part of the drivers, were riding northward out of the camp between the heavily rocking wagons, a scouting party of the enemy succeeded in setting fire to the broad, dry grass field on the mountain which rose to the east of the station, in order to deprive us of the good pasturage. The whole extent of the mountain flamed with red tongues of fire. In a fury, it flung itself like a red net over the field of bush; with broad front, it crawled more slowly down into the plain. The entire camp stood and looked at the pageant and railed at the injury which the enemy had done us.

Even the first day's march was very taxing. Now it led through bottomless sand, now over rough, stony ground. Many dead cattle, already skeletons or half devoured or in the early stages of decay, lay stinking right by the narrow track. Vultures circled over us and jackals howled in the bush. We rested toward night in a little church which was full of sick men. In the missionary's house, everything was smashed to bits, but over the door of the living-room there still hung a piece of pasteboard, on which were the words, "Love your enemies." In the little churchyard, not far from the church lay a long row of our men buried here in the last few months. On a captain's grave, there was a palm leaf certainly three yards long.

The higher we ascended the more frequently lay the dead animals by the road, and the worse was the pasturage. Wherever possible the enemy had cut the grass or burned it, and the rest our troops had used. Again, as before, we saw on the march not a house or permanent inhabitant; the only things we met were open columns returning to the camp, and once a single horseman. I happened to be the advance rider and hailed him familiarly, thinking he was a comrade or at the highest a non-commissioned officer. When he came nearer I saw, however, from his face, that he was a higher officer. He gave me a friendly reply and rode on. He was dressed like a private soldier.

This long, wearisome trekking through the broad, monotonous country devoid of human beings; this lying and smoking in the resting hours in the shade of the wagons, and the familiar, comfortable, slow talking,—teasing and a little bragging; this meagre food and scanty drink; a shot in the bush at a flock of partridges, or, if good luck would have it so, at an antelope; four hours' sleep by the flickering fire with my saddle under my head,—all this I was now experiencing again. And it seemed to me, now that I was for the second time on the road, as if I had known this country for a long, long time; as if long, long ago, before I was born, I had passed through a wild land beside a wagon and had slept and rested in its shelter. Such a feeling is due probably to the fact that these are the experiences of the forefathers, which sleep a long sleep through generations and again raise their hoary heads in the fancy of the child who is again led in the same ways and by-paths.

On the third evening, when we reached a water-place just at nightfall, we found a returning train of three wagons already camping there. They were just digging a grave, for one of the typhoid-fever patients whom they had brought had died. I sprang into the grave and made it half a yard deeper; they wouldn't wait any longer. Then we lowered him by bridle-straps fastened together, in his full uniform, and we laid his hat over his face. By his grave stood six Germans, burned brown, eight Boers, still browner, all wearing soft hats and high boots, and seventeen black men. The Boers shot over him. When his mother in a village in Pomerania held him on her lap, she did not dream that he would go to his grave so young, so far away, and with such a strange following.

When, late in the evening, we went over to the Boers' fire to ask them about the condition of affairs at the front, I noticed that a good dark brown horse was tied to the last wagon. I resolved to nab him for myself and began to look for an opportunity. We were to go on soon after midnight. When we were setting out, I sneaked back; but the Boers' dog barked and there was something stirring back of the wagon. I leaped away then, and a shot cracked behind me. The lieutenant and the others laughed at the long jumps I took. I was always on the lookout after that to see how I might capture a horse, for my Argentiner was induced to trot with more and more difficulty from day to day, and I knew from the many dead horses along our route that the front was badly provided with them. If I did not have a horse there, I should be only half a soldier, and above all I could not then reconnoitre.

At evening on the fourth day we overtook another provision column, which had been delayed by the oxen straying off. We rested for the night at the same water-place with this column and kept with it the next day.

The man who conducted this train had already been six years in the country. He had first been for three years in the home guard, then he had become a trader; that is, he had gone out from the railroad with an ox wagon and had travelled about in the interior toward the north, selling plug tobacco, coloured calico, and schnapps to the blacks, and getting his pay in calves and oxen. In Windhuk he had sold these to a wholesale dealer, but had always put a few out to graze in the care of a friendly farmer. He had already in this way gained for himself a considerable capital and had had the intention to go north once more, but this time to buy land in the neighbourhood of the friendly farmer. Then the whole black population round about him had revolted in furious hate against their hard, sly, foreign plunderers. He had saved himself with great difficulty, together with all his goods, to the souths and had enlisted now as a reserve.

I asked him many questions and he answered deliberately as he lay by the wagon with his short black *scheck*-pipe in his mouth. I asked him how he went about it to establish a farm, he replied:

"I hunt out a place with good pasturage and good water, then I get the government to allot me about five thousand hectares. It is not as exact as in Germany; the line would go from the tree to the water-hole, and then to the path, and so on. Then I let the few cattle that I own graze there, and they feed and water themselves and multiply just as in the time of Abraham and Jacob. After two or three years I have already a whole herd. Meanwhile I build myself a little stone house. When I begin by degrees to sell off a few cattle, I get a better house."

I asked him if in spite of the revolt and all the devastation he would stay in the country. He said:

"See! here you can go and stay and rest and trek a hundred miles and no one tells you what you are to do or not to do, and you have no anxiety about your neighbour on the next floor or across the hall, or about the paper in the living-room, or your daily bread. When you have eaten one calf, you kill another. If you don't care for veal any longer, you kill a goat. Or you go on a hunt as far as you please, three hours or three days, and if you don't get a shot just right at anything on the way, you tighten up your belt a little."

I asked if he would probably marry. He looked sidelong at me and said:

"When the war is over, a girl with whom I have entered into an understanding by correspondence is coming out. I know her parents and I know her a little, too. The farmers' wives here have a good time of it, you can believe,—little work, no envy and quarrelling, plenty of land, cows, and oxen, a horse to ride, and no anxiety about getting enough to live on."

So, he told me, and I was glad to hear it all; and I could perfectly understand all he said.

The bush was becoming somewhat less dense. Sometimes we would pass with our long train through a magnificent open plain; then again, our course would lead through thick bush so tall that one could, if need be, ride through it under the treetops, which touched each other. The days were clear and hot, as almost always in this country; the nights were cold, once so cold that our beards got icy and the water-sacks froze.

The further to the north we went, the more frequent were great tracts which the enemy had burned to take our pasturage from us. Every evening we saw a deep glow of fire to the north of us. Around the water-places the fields were bare for a considerable distance; the water was poor and had been polluted besides. More and more frequently horses which had collapsed and oxen which had got weak and had dropped in front of their wagons were lying in the road. Often, they used to make a fire behind these flabby oxen to get them up, but they lay there and died on the same spot. On the eighth day, there was a dead or dying animal every half-mile.

In the forenoon of the eighth day we saw not far to the north of us the elliptical balloon that floated in the air over the camp. So, at noon we rested only during the worst of the heat and then pushed on, reaching the camp at evening.

The men there were just at their cooking. In their high, yellow boots, full trousers, and shirtsleeves, they were sitting or bustling about the cooking-holes, and they called to us as we marched through to know if we had brought mail with us. They seemed to be in good spirits; the majority of them had, indeed, been only a month on land. In one corner was quartered a whole troop of Wittboys, hideous-looking men with wild, yellow faces. They had come from the south of our colony to help us, and wore our uniform and were commanded by German officers. In another corner, the great black horde of drivers were encamped around their fire, laughing and talking. Wagons and fieldpieces were standing around singly or in groups. But I was surprised the next morning to see how full the hospital was. I was surprised, too, at the horses; not that they had become rough from the cold nights, but that they were so thin and worn out. Many had in addition bad wounds around the mouth from the dry, sharp grass, and some had on their flanks great open sores covered with flies. Many of the men had lost their horses and were going on foot.

We were the centre division of the six great divisions which were coming upon the enemy in a half-circle in order to crush them, and for that reason we were the headquarters. That same evening, I saw the general addressing a scouting party, which then rode out into the night. He was a decided-looking, erect man, with grey hair and eyes.

We were no longer far from the enemy. Every reconnoitring party that was sent ahead and came back got sight of them. Some of these parties suffered severe losses, and one, led by a lieutenant, was entirely annihilated. I was glad to be again in a real army among so many cheerful soldiers, and I quite revived. Every day we practiced industriously in the bush, making sallies, slinking, and creeping through, and storming; we cleaned our arms, and did our mending and cooking. Once I was off all day long hunting strayed horses. I found them and appropriated one, a light brown East Prussian, and in exchange put my Argentine among those that I found. I think the lieutenant noticed it, but he didn't say anything. He had taken me into his company.

In the evenings, some of us who got on well together and liked each other used to gather under a wagon or by a cook-hole. Of my old comrades, I met only Gehlsen and Peters again, who were now wagon conductors in the staff guard. Among the new ones was one from Brunsbüttel.

I sat now among almost entirely new fellows and listened to their conversation. I had become more silent after all I had gone through, and from the extent and barrenness and heat of the land in which I had now lived for six months I had become slower and more apathetic than was really my nature. They used to like to talk about their former service or their homes or their callings. At last this one and that one came to speak of the reasons that had led them to enlist as volunteers for South Africa. Some wanted to stay in the army and get promoted faster. Some wanted to earn a little money from the war bounty in order to help their parents or to make themselves independent in their vocations. Many had been driven out by a youthful joy and enthusiasm, the Germanic desire for war and foreign parts. Some enlisted in order to see a bit of the world at the expense of the government.

Some, so it seemed to me, wanted to experience something about which they could boast for the rest of their lives. Some were silent as to the reasons which had impelled them; but those who knew them well said of one that he had had the misfortune accidentally to kill a schoolmate while playing with him, and of another that he had been thrown over by his sweetheart. These two were quiet fellows and often sat apart from the rest. But we talked mostly about the enemy, about their method of fighting, about their strength and intentions, and about the decisive blow that we wanted to inflict on them.

There were also among us some privates who had formerly been officers and had in some way lost their swords. As they might hope to regain their rank only in a war, they had longed for the outbreak of hostilities and had immediately applied as volunteers for the South West. Now they were common soldiers. One of these talked on the very first evening, with big words, a great deal about recognition of duty, self-discipline, sense of honour, and such things, so that I thought: "What an honourable man! How could he have lost his sword?"

But soon after and later I observed in the sand-field that he was making these speeches for himself, for he was always sulking and grumbling, especially at those who were set over him, from the non-commissioned officer up to the general himself, and he shirked every sort of work. Another was a lovable, helpful, and cheerful comrade whom we all liked and for whom we all wished the best. He was brave, too, at Hamakari. But he probably never attained his object, and if he had it wouldn't have been of much use to him, for when the chance came he forgot all his good intentions and drank and gambled like a madman. But the others—I heard about several of them—were brave men, good, simple soldiers, straight and silent in drill, like lions in a fight; and several of them fell, for only if they were severely wounded or mentioned for distinction did they win their swords again.

In another company, there was one fellow who had married young, so the story went, and had worked up to be first lieutenant. Two girls and then a little boy were born to him, and he was just mad with joy over the event. His old, inherited fault, which he had bravely held in control, raised its head; he got very drunk and was mixed up in a street brawl. So, he was dismissed, and now he was here in the South West. He sat alone a great deal, sunk into himself, never uttering a superfluous word. They said he never wrote to his wife and children. Everyone, officers and men alike, showed him consideration. But once, when in Okahandja a one-year volunteer came up to him with a glass of wine in his hand, and said to him good-naturedly, "To your youngest!" the unfortunate fellow, who seemed like one under a curse, gave him such a look that the volunteer stepped back with a pale face and an overturned glass.

Here I finally got a letter from home which had sought me a long time. They all wrote. Father wrote about the business; mother had talked to Dr. Bartels about how I could best protect myself against typhoid; the small sisters wrote about their new Sunday clothes. As I read their letters, I nursed the thought that I alone was grown up and that I had three such little sisters. It had never occurred to me till now. While I was still pondering over it, I looked up and saw by chance that a scouting party were coming home, covered with dust, their faces and hands lacerated with thorns. They were riding weary, wounded horses, and by their side they led two black prisoners tied with a rope. Then I realised where I was; I cast my daydreams into a corner and got up to look after my horse.

CHAPTER 13

A Dangerous Mission

As I had been longer in the country than the others, I received, on the fifth day after my arrival, a commission from headquarters to carry, with three men, a letter of instruction to the westerly division, which, as it was the last to arrive from Germany, was still somewhat behind in the march.

I arranged it so that the Mecklenburger got a better horse, and saw to it myself that the saddles were in good condition and that the necessary provisions and eight pounds of oats were in every saddle-bag. Then we rode out toward the west in the clear night. The first lieutenant had talked it all over with me explicitly,—the water-place, the trail, and the direction I was to take according to the cross which was clear in the heavens. I was to ride south as far as possible and then northwest, to see how far to the south the enemy was situated; but after a ride of about forty miles I was to turn back whether I had accomplished anything or not.

We rode briskly, first trotting the horses fifteen minutes and then walking them five. A blond boy, son of a Berlin cab-driver, rode ahead, then I myself and a young Alsatian, and behind us the man from Mecklenburg. It was a cold, clear, very bright night, not moonlight, but many stars shone brilliantly over the whole sky.

The first three hours passed without any special occurrence. The Berliner and I kept sharp watch in front and to the side. The Alsatian near me took strange positions in his saddle from time to time and confessed to me in a low voice that he had galled himself badly but had been very anxious to take the ride with us. The Mecklenburger trotted faithfully along in the sand behind us. It was so bright that I could see the dust thrown high by the horses' hoofs. Between the dull thuds of the hoofs on the sand sounded from a distance out of the bush the long, wailing howl of a jackal or the sharp laugh of a hyena, which startled me every time it suddenly occurred.

Sometimes a horse would stumble and his rider would pull him up again, swearing under his breath. Now and then a hoof would strike a stone so that it rang out sharply. To the northwest a bright glow of fire could be seen above the bush behind tall, distant trees. The Berliner maintained that he could smell a grass fire. The moon rose, and its clear, mild light lay soft and still, far over the bush. Somewhere about midnight, as we were trotting up a slowly ascending wagon trail, the Berliner raised his hand and pointed to the right in front of us across a clearing. Not five hundred yards from us, low on the ground, were glowing several little covered fires, like cats' eyes in the dark among the bushes.

As our horses snorted loudly, which they often did in the chilly night air,—and the night was bitter cold,—we dismounted quietly and led them awhile, spying in the meantime toward the fires on the right. We came soon to a place where the long grass was trodden down on both sides of the road. Getting down on my knees and creeping for a little way, I saw tracks of innumerable children's feet, and among them those of full-grown feet. Great troops of children, led by their mothers, had passed over the road here to the northwest. I stood up and, going to a low tree by the road, climbed up a few yards in my heavy boots.

Thence I could see a broad moonlit slope, rising not a hundred yards distant, and on it hundreds of rough huts constructed of branches, from the low entrances of which the fire-light shone out; and I heard children's crying and the yelping of a dog. Thousands of women and children were lying there under roofs of leaves around the dying fires. And away back of those, on the ever-broadening slope up to the foot of the mountains which reared their heights toward the blue, starry sky, stood more huts, like dark and indistinct lumps. The barking of dogs and lowing of cattle reached my ears. I gazed at the great night-scene with sharp, spying eyes, and I observed minutely the site of the camp at the base of the mountains. Still, the thought went through my head: "There lies a people, with all its children and all its possessions, hard pressed on all sides by the horrible, deadly lead, and condemned to death." and it sent cold shudders down my back.

We advanced cautiously, first on foot and then mounted. At six o'clock in the breaking morning light we came to a place with high, crisp grass, which the horses liked so much that we loosened their saddles and let them graze for an hour, while we stood by, the snaffles in our hands. At the right of the direction in which we were traveling rose steep in mighty bulk and strength like a rampart the extended mountain, in front of which the hostile people were encamped; the morning sun shone warm and bright on the forests lying on its ridge, and was driving away the mist which still hung on the corners of the woods. When we mounted again I noticed how stiff and tired our horses were, especially the horse of the Mecklenburger.

As we saw nothing more of the enemy, and as no tracks, except at most those of a single traveller, were visible on the road, I believed that we had the position of the enemy behind us. The Berliner thought so, too. So, we rode on for four hours, in continually increasing heat, and came then upon three deep water-holes in the limy soil, beside a tall tree. The Berliner threw in a stone and heard by the splash that there was water at the bottom. I talked it over with him and we decided we would have a proper noon rest here on the horses' account, for they were about at the end of their strength. We unsaddled, bound the snaffles together with the fodder bags on them, and let the Berliner go down and fetch up a little bad but cool water for the horses.

We didn't drink this water ourselves, but took the last of what we had in our water-sacks and filled them up with the bad water. Then we went to a tall tree to eat. I know still that the thought went through my head that we ought to stay in the burning sun because the tree stood too near the bush; but I allowed the others the cool shade and I didn't want the fellow from Berlin, who was rather conceited, secretly to think me cowardly; and I depended, too, on his alertness, for he was to hold the first watch. Meanwhile I undertook to watch the horses. I relate all this so minutely because I always nursed the idea that I neglected something.

When I had stood for probably two hours with the grazing horses, and was just going to stoop and kill a great, stinging fly that had lighted between the forelegs of my horse so that he was stamping violently, I heard from the clearing a short, frightful outcry, which seemed immediately to lay a hard pressure on my brain. Starting up, I saw that twenty or thirty of the enemy, armed with guns and clubs, were pressing round my comrades, who remained lying under the shots and blows. The Berliner, still half reclining, managed to shoot; but at the same moment that he held his gun to his cheek, he received such a fearful blow with a club that he sank back.

At that moment, too, came shots directed at me from the left across

80

the clearing. Loud shouts and abusive words filled the air. Leaping and creeping they came at me through the tall, waving grass. Then I sprang, with the snaffle still in my hand, upon the nearest unsaddled horse, got the tired beast into a gallop, and escaped along the bush.

I do not know much about the next hours. I only know that my head was horribly heavy and dull, as though my hat was full of lead, and that I held it strangely ducked down between my shoulders, keeping my eyes half closed and feeling all the time the terrible blows I had seen. I rode along probably three hours in a heavy stupor, brooding in a confused, half-crazy state. How and when I put the snaffle on my horse I do not know. It was that wretched animal which the Mecklenburger had ridden.

When I became a little clearer in my mind I bethought me of where I was riding, and I didn't know. I looked at the sun, but it was directly over me. Then I directed my course into the light wind which had blown up from the sea the night before, and rode toward that. I rode straight ahead all the time, but didn't come across a track or meet a human being.

I passed cleared places and through thick bush, which met over my head. My coat was in rags from the thorns, and my face and hands were bleeding. In order to spare my horse, I dismounted from time to time and led him, for he was overtired and suffering from thirst. Once when I had mounted again and was riding across a clearing, he stumbled and fell on his knees, and after resting awhile in that posture he fell over with a groan. I left him and went along on foot.

I took out my knife and bound it with a scrap of rope to my left wrist so as to have it ready when I could no longer use my gun. I preferred to take my own life rather than to fall alive into the hands of the enemy. When the knife was firmly fastened, I ventured to shoot three times, and listened for an answer; but none came. The sun was beginning to descend, and I saw now where the west was; but that didn't help me much, for I had no idea in what direction I had ridden the first few hours after the attack. My tongue lay heavy and thick in my mouth, my throat was dry down into my chest, and my thoughts were dull.

I thought I must die here so miserably and alone! How gladly had I lain instead with my dear friends under that tree in the far east! I tortured myself with thought of home, and in imagination gave each one my hand and said I was now about to depart this life and they mustn't grieve so very much,—life wasn't worth much any way; and I went to the first lieutenant and said he had trusted me in vain. I wasn't a clear-headed, calm fellow, but from childhood had been a dreamer. I wanted to speak a word to hear my voice, but I could not.

I went on, however, in my heavy boots, through sand and high, sparse, hard grass, climbed two or three times into trees or onto an ant-heap. Once I was startled by a great, heavy beast like an ox, only with two long horns standing straight up like a stag's horns. I didn't find out what sort of animal this was, for I never talked to anyone about those hours. Once in a while a gigantic dead tree would loom up before me. In the branches of one such hung a dark, thickly inter-woven mass as large and of the same shape as the body of an ox. In this lived numberless little grey birds. A thick black snake writhed slowly out of the nests and turned its head, hissing, this way and that, as if blinded by the sunlight. I ran on in a fright. Once I clambered up a rock that rose suddenly ten yards high out of the bush. I saw nothing, however, except smoke or sunlit dust in several places in the distance. Far and wide around me lay the silent bush.

Toward evening I came upon an indistinct, long-unused wagon trail. I rested not far from this, hidden in the bush,—for I thought someone might come along the road,—and I fell asleep. When I woke because I was so cold, it was dark. It was a clear, starry night like the preceding one. I stood up and looked about me in great distress and wished that I were dead.

Suddenly, while I was standing there, a vivid, sharp flash of light came over the bush diagonally before me. Again! and now again! A signal station; but how far off? Probably many, many miles. How bright it shone! There were comrades! There was salvation! It was madness to run to it; but I noticed the direction in the sky and ran as fast as I could.

I ran a good two hours or more, tearing my clothes and face and hands on the terribly long, hard thorns. Then I perceived that I was getting nearer, for the light was plainly beginning to flash higher above the bushes, but was too near to be coming down from a high, distant mountain. I shouted as loud as I could and ran on once more, but I soon gave that up. After running probably half an hour, I began shouting again, so that they should not shoot at me.

They were beginning to answer, "Come this way! Who are you? Come on!" I came out of the bushes and ran across the clearing to them where they were standing at the foot of jagged rocks, and told them who I was and what had happened to me.

"Poor devil!" they said. "We can be of very little help. We are sitting here ourselves in the worst case possible. Our under-officer, who understands giving the signals, went yesterday to the water-hole and didn't come back; and the corporal, who is now working the lamp, is sick. We have had no relief from duty for fourteen days; no sleep, no bread, only a little bit of rice, some canned meat, and water; and we are waiting for the blacks to come and finish us."

Two of the men had remained indifferent, lying wrapped in their cloaks. "They are sick," said the others.

I didn't hear what they were saying; I heard only the word water and begged for some. They gave me two covers full out of a water-sack, but it was vile tasting and I didn't take the third coverful. Meanwhile the corporal kept calling down from above to know who was there, and if relief had come. I observed from his speech that he was a Bavarian. The others said: "Go up and talk to him and cheer him up. He hasn't slept for two nights."

I climbed laboriously up the rocks and reached him. He was standing with his cloak on, taking the blinder off the lamp in correct time so that the flashes glared harshly out into the night. The light flickered in the icy-cold night wind. His whole body was shivering. Now he stopped manipulating the lamp and looked sharply over the dark bush toward a light that flashed out on the distant horizon, and he wrote rapidly on a block of paper what he saw. He asked me in broken sentences where I had come from and where I was going and said: "We are dirty and hungry and thirsty and sick, and two of us are already done for, but no one comes to relieve us."

I asked him: "Have you connections with the new division?"

He replied: "Just now in the last hour"; and he smiled mournfully and added: "I am going mad here. Yesterday night I signalled mere foolishness over and over: 'So we live, so we live,' and such things; but they didn't understand the nonsense." He let the block fall, crouched down and shook himself. He seemed to think that I was to relieve him.

I wanted to brighten him up, so I questioned him about the lights which flashed here and there in the darkness. He pulled himself together and pointed out to me with a nervous, hasty hand the light of each division. These lay in a half-circle around the enemy, ready to crush them on the morrow against the broad wall of the mountain in front of which they were encamped. While he was still showing me, a new light flashed down from the mountain. Vivid and bold, it suddenly appeared there.

"See!" he cried, "they have climbed up on the mountain. Now they are standing up there over the heads of the enemy, seeing everything and reporting what they see."

I gazed for a long time at the flaring light, and in spite of my own plight I thought of the ten or twenty comrades sitting up here on these unfriendly heights expecting every moment to be overwhelmed. And I looked at the broad, black stretch of land that lay dark among all the lights. There in the bush lay the hostile people. With what thoughts must they and their children see the light?

The Bavarian had again reached out to the lamp and wanted to pass on what he had received. He was talking softly to himself; then he sank down in a heap and again pulled himself up stiff. Just then we heard from out the bush the snorting of horses, and immediately after the sharp voice of an officer. I climbed hastily down and stood by, and heard him asking what the matter was here that such crazy messages had come. At that I stepped forward and explained that I was Corporal Moor; I told whence I had come and said that the Bavarian up there was sick and no longer quite in his right mind, and that I had lost comrades and horse and should like to go back to my division again.

He sent a man up the hill and said it wasn't necessary for me to take the dangerous ride again at once, for they now had signal connection once more with headquarters. But I said: "I have lost my comrades and I must report how it happened."

He probably had sympathy for me, for he said: "We have an extra nag among us. He is not beautiful, but if you want to go on, you shall have him." He went with me himself to the horse, and I believe he gave me a better one than he intended at first; for I heard him say in a low voice to his subordinate: "He has seven hours to ride and he is riding alone."

He looked after the saddle and bridle himself, and asked if I belonged regularly to the cavalry. Pulling at the girth, he said: "After three hours you must tighten the girth," and showed me the provisions for me and the horse in the saddle-bag. Then he called up to the hill: "Where are the headquarters?" They pointed them out, and he showed me the direction again by the Cross, which was clear in the sky, and instructed me to ride straight ahead till I came to the big path. With that he let me go.

On this ride, which lasted ten hours, I had no sort of accident. Dead tired I reached the road which my division were following, and, indeed, I drank and watered my horse at the place they had left two days before. I then took the same road they had taken. Many dead and dying animals lay along the road. At the next water-place I came upon the division resting. I announced myself, reported, and then went to my mess company, and sitting down on the ground slept like a dead man for six hours. They told me afterwards that they had besieged me with questions and I had looked at them without saying a word and had fallen back and slept.

That evening the camp was full of life. Everyone was busy. One was looking after his gun; another was carefully filling his cartridge-belt; a third was caring for his horse; a fourth and a fifth were lying on the ground, writing home. When we lay down to sleep around our cooking-hole, the volunteer, who was ten years older than we, said: "Well, boys, say 'Our Father' once more. Who knows if you'll be able to tomorrow night?"

No fire was lighted that night.

CHAPTER 14

The Flight of a Nation

Before midnight we advanced toward the enemy. It was said that our division would come upon them about morning. The Wittboys rode on ahead as spies. Then came our company. One part was detached to ride at the side of the road in the bush; the other part was to keep on riding in the road. I was in the third platoon. Behind me in compact array came the artillery. We marched as quietly as possible, but still there were all sorts of noises: snorting of horses, jolting of wheels, an impatient, angry shout, or a blow with a whip. I was very cold in the saddle, and, in order not to have stiff fingers later, when I had to shoot, I laid the reins over my cartridge-belt and put my hands in my pockets.

At last morning broke, and delicate, rosy stripes of light soon shot up toward the zenith. The colours grew rapidly deeper, brighter, and stronger. The red was glorious in its fullness and the blue beautiful in its purity. The light mounted and extended itself, ascending like a new world a thousand times more beautiful than the old one. Then came the sun, big and clear, looking like a great, placid, wide-open eye. Although like a good soldier I had all my thoughts fixed on what was before me, on the enemy, and the bad hours I should probably meet with, yet I saw the splendour of the sky.

Near me rode a fellow from Hamburg, a fresh, quiet boy. He said once to me: "You see, one has to have experienced something, or how shall one become a serious, capable man? That's why I came here." He was to enter his father's business later. He was riding just as I was, his reins over his cartridge-belt and his hands in his pockets; he was frowning this morning, and kept a sharp lookout before him. Diagonally behind me rode the former officer.

About this time of day, according to the predictions of our scouts, we ought to reach the enemy, but they were not to be seen. Then I thought, as did many others, that again there would be no fighting, and I was annoyed. Shortly after this, however, we heard the thunder of cannon coming from our right.

It got to be eight o'clock, and nine. The bush was so dense that the parties sent into it could not advance. They came out and marched together along the road. The sun was steadily mounting; it was getting to be a hot day. It began to be warm riding, and the horses were growing tired. A little thin lieutenant with a drawn face and sharp eyes rode up alongside of me and said, in a suppressed voice: "We aren't a mile and a half from the waterholes." Several times in the last few days he had made dangerous excursions into this region, and he knew every bush.

Then the first shot fell ahead. With a quick swing, we were out of our saddles and had thrown the reins over our horses' necks. Those who were to hold the horses seized them. Our company was only ninety strong, and, as we left ten with the horses, only eighty men went into the thick bush. The enemy were firing vigorously and letting out short, wild cries. I saw one of our men wounded. He stooped and examined a wound in his leg. Still, I saw nothing of the enemy. Then just for a second I saw a piece of an arm in a greyish brown cord coat, and I shot at it. Then I lay down to spy out another target. Lively firing was being exchanged. When one of us thought he had hit his mark, he would announce it with a loud voice: "That one won't get up again! I got him in the middle of the breast!"

The third man at my right, who was lying by a bush in front of me, twitched convulsively.

A derisive voice on the other side shouted: "Had enough, Dutchman?"

My comrade said, in a quiet voice: "I have a bullet in my shoulder," and he crawled back on all fours.

I could hear through all our own shooting that we were getting fired upon from the left. This fire now became heavier. They were coming nearer. In close ranks they came, creeping and shouting and screaming. Two of my neighbours were not shouting any more. We crawled back once or twice our length.

The enemy shouted: "Look out, Dutchman, look out!" and laughed wildly. Others shouted: "Hurrah! hurrah!"

The bush was swarming with men. I thought they would now break loose upon us in a wild storm and that it would be all up with us. On account of our wounded men I was fearfully anxious lest we should have to retreat. I was firmly resolved if the command should come, to shout loudly: "Take along the wounded!"

But when I had just decided on this plan, a subordinate officer came up with several men and cheered us on with the words, "Hold your position! I am sending aid!"

Soon afterwards I heard something slipping and grating behind me, and a quiet, soft voice said: "Move a little to the side."

The nozzle of a machine gun was pushed forward near my face, and immediately began to crackle away. The grape shot hissed furiously into the bushes rattling and whizzing. How good it sounded! How surely and quietly I shot! "Did I hit? Did you see? Shoot, man, there! there!" Cannon, too, upon a slope behind us were now thundering over our heads. Then it grew a little more quiet on the other side, and the command of "Forward, double quick!" reached us. We sprang up and plunged forward, but a horrible volley of grape shot was poured against us and threw us back again.

In front of me an under officer had got a ball in the body, and blood was streaming from the wound. He was crouching and trying to stem the flow of blood with a handkerchief, and was calling for help. He was a light-complexioned, fine-looking man. Just then the former officer, the one who was under the official ban, came up from the side, seized the wounded man by the shoulders, and dragged him back, while balls were falling around him and the barrel of his gun was hit so that it flew rattling to one side. He then quietly lay down in his place again. On the other side, in the bush, they were shouting in wild zeal and shrieking for very rage.

We did not advance. I don't know how long we lay there firing. It was probably hours. I wondered once why no officer was to be seen with us, and I forgot it again. Sweat ran like water over my entire body. Not merely my tongue, but my throat, my whole body, cried out for a swallow of cool water. At one side, a hospital aid was trying to bind a rubber bandage around the bleeding leg of a wounded man who begged him in South German dialect: "Take me back a little, can you?" Then the aid dragged him back panting.

The fire from the other side was getting weaker.

A voice commanded us: "Fire more slowly."

From the other side, we heard it jeeringly mimicked: "Fire more slowly."

A wounded man cried aloud for water.

We lay and waited, our guns pointed. Word passed from mouth to mouth: "The captain is dead; the first lieutenant, too—all the offic-ers—and almost all the under-officers."

Propping my gun in position, I took my field flask with my left hand and swallowed the little draught I had saved up for the greatest emergency. As I set the flask aside, I thought that perhaps it would be my last drink, and I thought of my parents. I believed that the enemy would get breath and then make another assault.

But that did not happen. A lieutenant who belonged to the staff came stooping along our ranks. When he was behind me, he knelt there, touched my boot lightly, and said; "Go to the general and report that according to my reckoning we are about half a mile distant from the last water-holes."

I got cautiously up on my knees, and then ducking down ran back to the road. Near an ant-hill, which was certainly three yards high, a surgeon and a hospital aid were endeavouring to save a man from bleeding to death; but I believe they came too late, for he lay like dead on his dark red blanket. Then I saw the balloon not far in front of me and I ran across the clearing to it.

The long rows of oxen, standing in harness in front of their wag-ons, raised their open mouths and bellowed hoarsely, for they scented the water-holes and panted for water. The soldiers at the wagons and horses called to me with dry voices: "Get ahead, you fellows up for-ward! Are we coming to water soon? Are we going on?" They looked at me with deep, dry eyes. Those who held the horses had a great deal of trouble with the thirsty creatures, which were standing crowded to-gether, swarmed over and tortured by insects. The sun scorched down. A thick, horribly dry, dust-filled air lay over the whole camp.

The surgeons in white cloaks stood in front of the hospital wagon around a table on which someone was lying. I wondered how many were lying in the shade of the wagon; five or six of them were dead, among them our captain. A wounded officer, I think it was a lieuten-ant, was giving water with his well hand to the severely wounded; his other arm was bleeding badly.

At the general's wagon, a man was standing by the heliograph. The general was nearby with officers and orderlies around him, all of them on foot. I reported and heard someone say: "The animals can't hold out any longer and the men are simply dying of thirst." The next mo-ment, just as I had turned to run to the front, there came from behind from two or three directions wild shouting and volleys from the bush.

The outposts, who were lying and kneeling on the ground all

around, moved in immediately. The voice of an officer rang out sharp and clear: "Disperse and charge in knots." I ran, and saw as I ran that a hailstorm of bullets was riddling the hospital wagon, that the doctors were seizing their guns, and that one of them was wounded. I even heard one say: "We'll take off our white cloaks, though." Then I lay down by a bush and shot at the enemy, who with wild shouts continued their onset through the bushes. Secretaries, orderlies, drivers, guard, and officers all rushed forward, lay down near one another, and protected their skins. The artillery turned while firing and shot away over us. Excited by my run and the sudden attack, I began a violent, rapid fire.

A voice near me said: "Shoot more calmly." I did fire more calmly, thinking, "Who said that?" and as I seized my cartridge-belt and looked to the side, there lay the general two men from me, shooting coolly as becomes an old soldier. The enemy were pressing on in close ranks through the bush, shouting and firing. But we lay quietly and shot well. Then it got more quiet. The officers stood up and returned to the centre of the camp again. Immediately after that came the order that the whole camp should advance two hundred yards. In running by I saw them lifting the dead and wounded into wagons. Then I ran forward again to my place in the line of defence.

Now as I lay there I felt how very parched I was. Begging and complaining and teasing for water went through the ranks. From behind we heard the hoarse lowing of the thirsty oxen. I believe that at this time, four in the afternoon, there was not a drop of water in the whole camp except for the wounded.

Then everything was moved to the front,—soldiers, artillery, and machine guns. A terrific fire rattled against the enemy, who were growing weary. Then word passed from man to man: "We are going to charge." Now the battle-cry told. I shall never forget it. With fierce yells, with distorted faces, with dry and burning eyes, we sprang to our feet and hurled ourselves forward. The enemy leaped, fired, and dispersed with loud outcries. We ran without interference, shouting, cursing, and shooting, to the good-sized clearing where the ardently desired water-holes were, and across it to the further edge, where the bush began again.

The entire camp—the heavy wagons with their long teams of oxen; the hundreds of horses; the hospital wagons with the surgeons, the dead and the wounded; the headquarters, everything—followed in a rush and encamped in the clearing. But we lay around it at the edge of the bush to keep back the enemy, who now here and now there would break through the thick bushes in wild, loudly shouting parties. Behind us our men were now climbing down with army kettles into the water-holes, which were ten yards deep, and were filling buckets let down on reins and were beginning to water man and beast. When about ten animals had had a little, the hole was empty. There were about ten or twelve holes at this place.

The sun went down. Some of us slipped out, cut brush with our side-arms, and made a stockade in front of us. The artillerymen set up the cannon and machine guns behind us and knelt near them. Some of the soldiers were detailed to creep from man to man and give each a little water. In the camp further back of us, the restlessly crowding animals were being watered in the dark. By the hospital wagons nurses were going about, lanterns in their hands, bending over each patient. Meanwhile the enemy kept up their firing, which continually flashed out of the dark bush all around the camp. Not until about midnight did it become more quiet. We passed a little *zwieback* from hand to hand. Then complete darkness settled upon us and the shooting at last ceased.

What plan had the enemy in mind? Here we lay in the dark night, four hundred men, worn out, and half dead with thirst; and in front of us and all around us a savage, furious people numbering sixty thousand. We knew and heard nothing of the other German divisions. Perhaps they had been slaughtered and the sixty thousand were now collecting themselves to fall upon us. Through the quiet night we heard in the distance the lowing of enormous herds of thirsty cattle and a dull confused sound like the movement of a whole people. To the east there was a gigantic glow of fire. I lay stretched at full length with my gun ready, and cheered my utterly exhausted comrades to keep awake.

Thus, morning gradually came on. Then some scouts went out cautiously and we learned to our great amazement that the enemy had withdrawn, and indeed in wild flight. We should have liked to follow them up, but we had no news yet from the other divisions. Moreover, both men and beasts had reached the limit of their strength. So, we rested on that day, ate a little poor food, and cleansed and repaired our guns and other equipment; for we looked like people who had battered and bruised and soiled themselves in an attack of frenzy. The madness still showed in our frowning brows and in our eyes. Our dead lay in the midst of us in the shade of a tree.

We had a great deal of trouble to keep our animals from dying. We could not give them anywhere near enough water to satisfy them, and we could not give them any fodder at all, because the entire region had been eaten as bare by the enemy's cattle as if rats and mice had gnawed it clean. The men and the animals had even grubbed into the earth in search of roots. It was a miserable day. The sun glared down, and an odour of old manure filled the whole land to suffocation.

At noon there came at last some news from the other divisions. Two reported that they had beaten the enemy, the third that it had saved itself with great difficulty and distress. The enemy had fled to the east with their whole enormous mass,—women, children, and herds.

Toward evening we buried our dead under the tree.

CHAPTER 15

A Dry and Thirsty Land

The next morning, we ventured to pursue the enemy. We left our unmounted men with the sick and wounded in camp and set out towards the east, two hundred horsemen in number. But our horses were weak, half-starved, or sick, and the region into which we were advancing was a waterless land and little explored. The ground was trodden down into a floor for a width of about a hundred yards; for in such a broad, thickly crowded horde had the enemy and their herds of cattle stormed along. In the path of their flight lay blankets, skins, ostrich feathers, household utensils, women's ornaments, cattle, and men dead and dying and staring blankly. A shocking smell of old manure and of decaying bodies filled the hot, still air oppressively.

The further we went in the burning sun, the more disheartening became our journey. How deeply the wild, proud, sorrowful people had humbled themselves in the terror of death! Wherever I turned my eyes lay their goods in quantities: oxen and horses, goats and dogs, blankets and skins. And there lay the wounded and the old, women and children. A number of babies lay helplessly languishing by mothers whose breasts hung down long and flabby. Others were lying alone, still living, with eyes and noses full of flies. Somebody sent out our black drivers and I think they helped them to die.

All this life lay scattered there, both man and beast, broken in the knees, helpless, still in agony or already motionless; it looked as if it had all been thrown down out of the air. At noon, we halted by water-holes which were filled to the very brim with corpses. We pulled them out by means of the ox-teams from the fieldpieces, but there was only a little stinking, bloody water in the depths. We tried to dig deeper, but no water came. There was no pasturage, either. The sun blazed down so hot on the sand that we could not even lie down. On our thirsting, starving horses, we thirsting and starving men rode on. At some distance crouched a crowd of old women who stared in apathy in front of them. Here and there were oxen, bellowing. In the last frenzy of despair man and beast will plunge madly into the bush, somewhere, anywhere to find water, and in the bush, they will die of thirst.

We rode on till evening. Then we expected to reach a dry river bed and find water nearby. Herds of beeves, bellowing hoarsely and with wild, gleaming eyes, came towards us in a cloud of dust. That was a bad sign of the region into which we were riding. "Do you think you are wiser than the animals? Turn back, turn back!"

"No, we know better. At seven we shall reach the enemy, and water and pasture."

We kept on. Our ranks became straggling. We rode each one of us as best he could. There was nothing to be seen of the enemy, but Wittboys who had ridden on ahead came back and reported that their camp was not far off.

Toward evening, when I was ordered to ride in the bush with four men as a flank protection,—for we were shot at now and then,—we chanced to see a Cape wagon behind some high bushes, and we heard human voices. Dismounting, we sneaked up and discovered six of the enemy sitting in animated conversation around a little camp-fire. I indicated, by signs, at which one of them each of us was to shoot. Four lay still immediately; one escaped; the sixth stood half erect, severely wounded. I sprang forward swinging my club; he looked at me indifferently. I wiped my club clean in the sand and threw the weapon on its strap over my shoulder, but I did not like to touch it all that day.

The ground was everywhere bare, yellowish brown and stony; the sparse grass had been eaten, burned, or trodden down. Dead cattle lay about everywhere. The hoarse bellowing of dying oxen quavered horribly through the air. The bush got thinner, often opening into a great clearing.

Entirely forsaken in the scorching sun lay a two-year-old child. When it caught sight of us, it sat up straight and stared at us. I got down from my horse, picked the child up and carried it back where there was a deserted fireplace near a bush. It found at once the remainder of a root or a bone, and began to eat. It did not cry; it did not show fear, either; it was entirely indifferent. I believe it had grown there in the bush without human help.

The hot day was drawing to a close. Our horses were very tired. We had trouble to get the creatures up again when they stumbled.

Some of us dismounted, and by evening many were leading their horses. Then the animals fell, and their riders threw the saddles into the wagons and continued on foot. It grew dark; still nothing was to be seen of the enemy. Then at last we reached the eagerly longed-for water-holes. There they were, filled to the very top with dead oxen. No water was there; no trace of fodder. Then we bit our lips and stared ahead of us, for we knew now that we must go back and that many more horses would fall. We might be happy indeed if we brought all our men back to the camp alive.

We stayed here three or four hours in the night. I tried to get a little water by forcing my way down between the dead cattle and oxen, and after an hour came back with half a kettleful of the vile liquid. We made coffee with it, however, and drank it. The others in the meantime had got a great rough nest of weaver birds from a tree and had laid it before the horses; we gathered old cow-dung, too, and cut branches from the bushes and offered them those after removing the thorns. I stayed an hour by my horse, rubbing him with my hand and being friendly with him.

After midnight, we started on our return journey. At first, when a horse fell the rider would take the saddle on his back and trudge in his heavy boots through the sand, but soon the saddles lay scattered all along. We others dismounted and led our horses; it was a long, weary procession. Right under my feet a comrade staggered and fell; four of us lifted him up,—he was heavy as lead. More horses were falling all the time. Soon a noble beast was left lying every half-mile. Now and then a shot cracked, but we paid no attention. The older carcasses were distended; a terrific atmosphere exhaled from the broad field of death. We set one foot before the other in silence.

Our mouths were hot; the suffocating, vile-smelling air passed down our throats like whips and spurs. One man in front of me began to talk wildly, saying he wanted to kill all the enemy and drink himself full of their blood. We put him on a horse and two men held him. I felt no hunger,—loathing drove away hunger,—but I was tortured by thirst, so that I longed to drink the blood which I saw in the veins of the fallen animals.

Morning came and with it the burning sun. We came to water-holes, again full of dead cattle. Nevertheless, we threw ourselves down and tried to get water out of the bottom, and we filled a cover with the repulsive stuff and drank in turn. When my turn came and I was already raising the cover to my mouth, my head was pushed gently aside. As I looked around in amazement, my horse stuck his nose into the cover and drank. I forced myself to preserve my self-control and thought: "Do you want to drink death in spilt blood? Better die of thirst." And I let him have it and stood up, no longer having any hope of holding out till the evening of that terrible day. Our line got longer and longer.

It is wonderful how much a human being can endure. I walked four hours more in the burning sun. I know little or nothing of those hours; I have only a recollection of having passed through a flaming fire. My horse fell and lay there.

Towards evening, when we were still five miles distant from the camp, I was ordered to mount another horse and try to see if I could reach there in order that they might send out fresh oxen to meet us, for our teams refused to go on. I climbed into the saddle and actually got the East Prussian horse into a slow, heavy trot. So, I rode alone along the path of death.

When I had ridden awhile, a thick, dark cloud, like a thunder-cloud, came up from the south. I rejoiced at the sight and watched greedily as it grew broader and broader and broader; I almost believed I could taste the rain already. Then it struck me that it hung very low and approached very rapidly, exactly as if it were flying. And now it was upon me. Whirring and humming, a numberless swarm of big grasshoppers buzzed thick about me. Their shining, silver wings, which were as long as my finger, glittered with marvellous beauty in the setting sun. They settled in countless numbers about me on the bush. I shook myself in horror of this wonderful, fearfully strange land, and passed through them. I reached camp and reported; I drank, dropped down, and slept.

CHAPTER 16

The Limit of Endurance

During the four days that we still remained in this camp, we had the flesh of the oxen which had given out and rice for our three meals a day; there was no other food. There was, to be sure, water enough for the time being; but as the hordes of the enemy with their great herds of cattle had lived for weeks around these same water-holes, the water had become badly polluted. Thus, it happened that in a few days every tenth man fell sick of dysentery. I kept fairly well, but once, when searching under a bush for a little grass for my half-starved horse, I got wounded by a thorn in my hand, which swelled up and looked bad for some days. Apparently the whole place was infected,—the water, the ground, the bush, and the air.

Then came the news that the enemy, after overcoming and passing the great stretch of waterless country, where thousands of them had perished, were situated far to the east on the further side of the sand field by some miserable water-holes. The general decided to follow them thither, to attack them and force them to go northward into thirst and death, so that the colony would be left in peace and quiet for all time.

We now advanced into broad *steppes* to the east, marching, as was our usual method, with an immense baggage train of ox-teams, Cape wagons, carts, and drivers, which carried along all our means of supporting life in the desert. Of these *steppes*, where no white man before us had ever trod, little was known except that they were very poorly supplied with water. On the way, a large supply of fresh horses reached us, so we were all mounted again. It was the fourth horse I had ridden, and the lieutenant, who had been on many and long reconnoitring expeditions, was mounting his sixth. We were four hundred men in our division.

The sand was deep and the sun was scorching. At night, lying on the ground, our heads pillowed on our hats or saddles, we got a little sleep. The stars were clear, and an icy wind blew. The food was monotonous and meagre. Many had drunk the seeds of typhoid fever in the infected water, and the disease now broke out. The sick men had to ride back all day on the floors of the hard, jolting wagons until they came to a field hospital, where they would lie for weeks on miserable grass beds without proper food to strengthen them, without drink to cool their fever, and without cleanliness.

The further on we penetrated into the *steppes*, the more troublesome became the big flies which always come at this time of year, and which were so rapacious that we had to pick them out of our eyes and the corners of our mouths with our fingers. That they were always floating in our soup had long since ceased to bother us. In the second or third week, the new horses began to get exhausted. Soon one, and then another, was lying by the way. The oxen, from long marches and poor fodder, were getting more and more flabby. Our clothes, boots, saddles, and harness were again torn and dirty. We looked as if we had rolled in the dust.

When we had marched three weeks and had reached the region where the enemy were supposed to be, it appeared that they had gone still further east and were stopping at the very last of the wretched water-holes. So, we had to go still further. At night, we would see here and there to the east of us the burning grass which they had set on fire, and the fires of the single tribes which had detached themselves from the main body and were trying to break through to the west, to their old home, in order to escape a cruel death from thirst. Scouting parties were sent out to prevent their getting through, so that they should not keep up an endless petty warfare with us in their native district.

At last, in the fourth week, I again left the company. I rode with a party of twenty men, led by a lieutenant, out of the night camp to the north in order to get information about this region, of which there was no map, and more especially to find some good water. There were in the vicinity, to be sure, many water-holes; but two out of three would be found dried up and the third would contain miserably little water.

We set out after midnight and rode till nine o'clock in the morning. Then we unsaddled to rest. But we had not been lying long in the shadow of some bushes when we noticed an odour of something burning, which grew rapidly stronger, so that we thought it right, in spite of our indifference, to investigate the cause. Just then our outposts came running up and said that the wind was driving a mighty grass fire toward us. Cursing the enemy, we got up and saddled in haste, for heavy smoke and fire which gleamed through it were coming toward us in a broad front.

As our horses were getting restless and were rearing and plunging into one another, we walked as fast as we could, leading them without any concerted action toward a depression in the cleared ground. We had just reached it and were beginning to cut and tear up the grass for a little space, when the flames came up like a tribe of little glowing children who were dancing forward holding each other's hands. Here and there one would spring up higher than the rest and immediately duck down again. They roared as they crept along, blowing a dry, hot breath before them which they drove into our mouths and eyes. Some of us had poured some of the cold coffee which we had in our water-sacks on our handkerchiefs, others crouched down behind their horses, and others pressed their faces against the moist water-sacks.

Then there was a moment of great confusion: the horses reared wildly; our breath stopped; a comrade stumbled and was pulled up again—then it was past. We looked like chimney-sweeps; and we cursed and shook our heads and looked at one another; and at last we had to laugh over the adventure. But I especially laughed to myself at the thought of that rascal from Holstein who had sometimes, as he said, been shoved by his mother into the oven. I would not have begrudged him this adventure.

In the evening, we reached some dried-up water-holes, which we dug somewhat deeper and by which we slept that night, laying our saddles in a circle and each man lying behind his own. The horses were enclosed in a pretty good grazing-place by thorn branches which had been hastily cut and gathered together. The lieutenant and the officer who had lost his commission took turns watching in the circle of sleeping soldiers. Two guards, who were relieved every hour, walked outside the circle, and one man stood with the horses.

When it came my turn to watch and I went outside, the night was so bitter cold that I made all sorts of motions to keep a little warmth in my body. I even climbed twice on a low, tumble-down anthill and watched the fires which here and there in the distance shone through the darkness. While I was thus gazing, however, I was struck by the fact that one fire was burning not far from us in the thick bush. I remembered it when I was relieved, and told the lieutenant, who was sitting on the ground by our burned-out fire.

Before dawn we got up, discovered the exact place in the bush, and stealthily surrounded it. Five men and eight or ten women and children, all in rags, were squatting benumbed about their dismal little fire. Telling them with threats not to move, we looked through the bundles which were lying near them and found two guns and some underclothing, probably stolen from our dead. One of the men was wearing a German tunic which bore the name of one of our officers who had been killed. We then led the men away to one side and shot them. The women and children, who looked pitiably starved, we hunted into the bush.

When we got back to the place where we had spent the night, so much water had trickled into the holes which we had deepened that we could give a whole cook-pan full to every horse and put a little in our water-sacks besides. The water was not so bad as regards taste, but, as was almost everywhere the case in that sandy soil, it contained a considerable proportion of *Glaubersaltz* and had, therefore, what the lieutenant called a decidedly laxative effect.

All that day, to the great vexation of the lieutenant, we found no good water-place, but we continually rejoiced to be out of the company and traveling alone through the broad, boundless country. While we were riding, the lieutenant described to us his plan of hunting up our nearest little post, which had already been camping somewhere in the vicinity for several weeks in order to prevent the return of the hostile tribes to their homes. At this post, he was going to make inquiries. But towards evening, before, according to our information, we could possibly have arrived at that post, the bushes began to be more luxuriant and the grass softer; some tall trees rose from the bush and some fowl flew up.

In short, we noticed that we were coming to water, and, feeling very happy and proud at our cleverness in discovery, we put our horses into a trot. And, behold, there at the side of a clearing was truly a little pond, or rather puddle, of clear water. We came up, dismounted, and some were already kneeling and drinking and the horses were standing knee-deep in the water near us when just then a strange soldier came running towards us down a hill, shouting: "For Heaven's sake, don't drink that water! Don't drink! There's typhoid fever in it!"

We stopped and shrugged our shoulders. Some of the men were serious, some laughed indifferently. Above, on the slope, was a newly established army hospital which we had not known of. We spent the night nearby, apart from the typhoid patients and the miserable pond, however. But with this water, as appeared after some weeks, six of us had drunk in typhoid fever and two of us death.

The next morning, we made a very early start, and at about ten o'clock found the post we were in search of. Fifteen soldiers were living in a cleared space, in a little camp which they had fortified with a barricade of thorn-bush. Inside this barricade they had built two huts of branches and had made a big cooking-hole. Outside, at some distance, were their horses, and cattle, namely, four cows, which they had seized and from which they got milk. To do the milking and washing and to gather wood they had captured an oldish bush-woman.

The lieutenant in command of the post was a thickset man with reddish hair, on account of which and because he was so untiringly active and ingenious in spying out and holding up wandering hostile bands, he had won the name of "The Red Freebooter." He was just returning from such an expedition. If his mother, the wife of a burgo-master, could have seen him, she would have been horrified. His head was shaved as bald as a rat, his beard was stubbly, his coat filthy, his trousers badly torn, and his boots trodden down. Half a dozen pearl fowl, which he had shot on the way back, hung by a strap of fresh ox-hide over his shoulder, and when he afterwards opened his coat a little I observed that on that day at least he was wearing no shirt. It was probably in the wringing hands of the spindle-legged bush-woman. He was very glad to see us, and, making fun of himself, told us about his present importance and his efficiency. Then he invited us to dinner.

It was always the same when we met comrades from another division. We always talked on three subjects: first, the enemy; second, the events in the army; and, third, the various ways of cooking. After topics, first and second had been sufficiently discussed, our host, with an important manner, led us to a place in the corner of the camp where a little thin smoke was issuing out of the ground. He took a piece of wood and carefully pushed aside the earth.

Then appeared to our view two cooking-pans packed around with dry cow-dung which was smouldering a little. Two men came up and with great skill lifted from the hole the pans, which, the lieutenant informed us, had been standing in this heat for sixteen hours. Then he took off the cover and with great pride invited us to smell of the contents of the pans. It was a fine soup and the meat was well cooked, too. We had to praise it highly and we also liked it, but we were somewhat depressed that they and not we had made this great discovery.

While we were sitting around, each one with his pan-cover in his hand, the red lieutenant gave us another surprise in the shape of a rather recent number of a South African newspaper. As it had already passed from hand to hand in this camp, it had become somewhat dirty and ragged. Still our lieutenant clutched it eagerly, spread it out, and looked, whether by chance or not, at the place where the new decorations are announced. Then looking up suddenly at the reduced officer, who was sitting as usual a little apart from us and staring at the ground in front of him, he called him by name and said: "Comrade, look here!" The man started out of his reverie and came and knelt down behind the lieutenant, looking at the place which the latter pointed out. Then he began to breathe short and hard. The lieutenant looked at us and said softly: "He has just been suggested for decoration."

At that the ex-officer could no longer hold back the violent sobs which he had been repressing. He wept, and we pressed around him and grasped his hand, our own eyes wet. Then he wrote a postcard to his wife and children and we had to sign our names: a linen-weaver from Upper Schleswig, a chimney-sweep from Berlin, a farm hand from Oldenburg, a Bavarian count, a locksmith's apprentice from Holstein, and others.

We were all in a state of excitement over this occurrence when a guard came in from the cattle and reported: "*Herr Lieutenant*, the brindle cow wants to calve and can't."

The red lieutenant looked much perplexed. "What!" said he, "Can't! Of course, she can."

Then we all laughed at him and were very jolly, and the farm hand from Oldenburg helped the cow.

After that we rode on. The red lieutenant knew nothing of any good water-place; he said we must get used to going without water.

In the afternoon, on the way back to our division, we overtook a provision train, with the leader of which our lieutenant talked for a while. The others chatted meanwhile with the guard, but I could not take my eyes off a driver who walked along near his oxen with long, dignified strides, his whip over his shoulder. Behind him walked his wife with a little two-year-old child in a shawl on her back. Then came still in single file, graduated according to height, three more half-grown children. A pipe, the common property of the family, went from the man all along the line to the last little eight-year-old, who, after he had had a few pulls, took it back on the trot to his father. Only the smallest had not yet any interest in the pleasures of tobacco.

From his seat on his mother's back he was trying, with some success, I believe, to reach her breast, which hung down long and flabby.

As I rode along still reflecting on this picture, the lieutenant called me and told me that, according to the story of the leader of the column, the head doctor, sick himself, and with a single sick companion and a black servant, had passed on this road about an hour before in order to reach our division; but now no more of their tracks were to be seen and it was feared that they had followed another path, which would not lead to a water-place. I was to ride on with two men in search of them and escort them to the division.

I was much pleased with this commission and fulfilled it with especially good luck; for when we had ridden about an hour, during which time I had examined, like an old hunter, every track which crossed our path, I discovered to my great joy that three riders had turned off the path, to the right, at a place that was sandy enough to show their track plainly. They were evidently trying to reach the camp by the shortest way, straight across the bush. We followed their course and soon saw the three lonely riders going along in front of us in the thin bush on their very weary horses.

On the left rode the doctor, recognizable by his short, sturdy figure; I had seen him several times before the last fight. His companion, who was riding at the right, hung in the saddle as though he were asleep; now and then the doctor reached over to him as if to hold him or shake him up. The black servant rode as leader some twenty yards in advance. I shook my head in disapproval of the way the doctor had to ride with such a scanty escort and protection from hospital to hospital straight across this pathless, waterless country overrun by hostile tribes, and I put my tired horse into a trot. Therefore, the black servant looked around and announced our approach. The doctor again gave his companion a cuff, turned his horse, and took his gun out of its rest.

Since many of the enemy used to wear our uniforms and hats, and since our sunburned faces looked almost black, especially as the sun shone nearly vertically down on us, he took us for the moment for foes; but when we took off our hats, he recognised us. I now saw that the other man was very sick and could no longer hold himself properly in the saddle, and that the doctor himself, who at the fight four weeks before had looked well and fresh, was very much worn, and looked wearily and feverishly out of deep-sunken eyes. For the last six weeks, he had ridden from one division to another, and yesterday and today had covered about forty miles; and he had not slept for twenty hours. While he was asking me where I came from and where I was going, and was drinking out of my water-sack, scolding the while at his black servant, who out of sheer indifference and laziness had not filled his water-sack, my men were helping his escort down from his horse. Soon by main force they lifted him back into his saddle and we rode slowly on again.

Late in the evening we arrived dead tired at our division, which was spending the night by some dried-up water-holes. It was a very cold, unpleasant night. A sharp, cutting wind blew across the *steppes* and drove fine, dry sand over the thirsting men and animals.

The following day we were overtaken by a thunder-storm. Dark clouds rose as if from all sides at once, heavy thunder rolled over the broad plain, gleaming whips of lightning quivered across the whole sky, and rain poured in torrents. But after one hour all dampness was gone and a stormy wind blew the sand into our faces so that we could not open mouth or eyes. We protected ourselves in bivouac from the biting cold by putting up canvas as a screen against the wind. Behind this shelter we cooked our daily fare of tough meat and rice with bad water over a miserable fire. We talked little and gloomily. Far in the east were great clouds of smoke and flame. The enemy on their retreat into the desert were burning the sparse, dry fodder.

The next forenoon we expected to find water at a place near the dried bed of a river. We found holes, but they were empty. Twenty men got down into them and dug them deeper, but no water came. So we could neither drink nor cook. The horses, too, could not graze without being watered first, for their parched mucous membranes could not digest the dry, coarse grass. There was nothing to do but go on. We dismounted, and, leading our horses, walked in a long weary train through deep, blowing sand, under hot sun, with burning throats. Occasionally a horse stumbled and his owner pulled him up again and talked to him kindly or roughly. In this way night came on and it grew dark. The ground was stony and we could no longer see the trail.

We halted, stationed sentinels about us, lighted a few fires, and lay sleeping heavily on the ground. Our horses stood or lay near us by the fires.

About midnight the moon rose slowly over the broad *steppes*. We called in the sentries, saddled, and went on; and after three hours were close to the water-place which our scouts had found in reconnoitring. The moonlight was so brilliant that we could see the waterholes from a long distance lying like dark spots in the ghostly white limy surface.

At one side stood single beautiful tall trees with two grey ant-hills bright in the moonlight. It looked like a splendid square, paved with marble, in the midst of a magnificent park, with statues under tall, still trees at one side of the square. The horses raised their heads and quickened their gait, and their sleepy, half-starved, cold riders came to life.

The leaders of our party were now at the first water-hole; but their horses turned away and went to the second and the third. Then the rest of us came up and noticed the odour of carrion, which, like a wicked, hidden monster, lay flat over the whole beautiful moonlit clearing, ready to devour us. The holes were full of decaying cattle. The horses stood there with drooping heads, and we near them, propping ourselves up on our guns. Many a one, dead with sleep and weak from hunger, swayed as he stood.

We had to go on to make use of the cool of the night. Then many a one thought: "If I had only stayed at home! If I could be at home now, never again would I go away!"

But his stumbling horse waked him out of his dream. And then after a few more faltering steps the poor animal would fall forward on his knees and lie there groaning. The rest would pass indifferently by him and his prostrate horse, and then it meant: "Don't stand there so long! Quick! Take off the bag and sling it over your own shoulders!"

At that he would get wide awake, as if someone had said: "Behind you and on both sides under the dry bushes follows and lurks Death. Ahead, and there only, is life and a return home." He would stoop for the pack, take one more look into the eye of his horse, and trudge on.

Along the path lay many little burnt-out fires, and near them all sorts of abandoned goods belonging to the enemy or stolen by them, especially clothes and saddles and Christian books which the missionaries had given or sold them. The whole way was bestrewn with cattle which had fallen dead. We had reached the path of the enemy's flight. A reconnoitring party came up with the news that our other division had surprised a part of the foe, pelted them with shell, and dispersed them.

The next day we at last reached a good water-place and here joined the other division. Combining our forces, we were now going to attack the enemy, who were at the next and last water-place, and deal them a finishing blow. It was the general belief that there would be a battle just as severe and with as great loss as the one four weeks before. The general, wishing to see the united divisions all drawn up in battle array and also wishing to raise their spirits in expectation of battle, ordered a parade and religious services for the next day.

We took up our positions in the broad clearing,—the horsemen, those who had to go on foot, and the artillery with the cannon. The oxen, the black drivers, the Cape wagons, and the sky over the wide steppes looked on. We stood in beautiful order, and it sounded very magnificent, the "Good-morning, soldiers!" "Good-morning, your Excellency!" But the horses were thin, shaggy, and weary; our clothes and boots were torn; and hunger and sickness stared many of us in the face.

At four in the afternoon we assembled for the service. The chaplain had been with the other division all the time, so that I had seen him for the first time only a few days before. He was a big, strong man, and wore a uniform and high boots, just as we did. He sat in the saddle with his gun by his side and his cartridge-belt around his waist. Even now when he stood before the chest, which was covered with a red cloth, he was in uniform and riding boots; but he had a gold cross hanging on his breast and wore on his arm a blue and white band with a red cross on it. First, we sang the song, "We come to pray before a just God." Then he began to speak. He said that a people savage by nature had rebelled against the authorities that God had set over them and besides had stained themselves with revolting murders. Then the authorities had given the sword, which we were to use on the morrow, into our hands. Might every man of us use it honourably, like a good soldier! It was a serious hour. It might well be that one or another would not live till the next night. We would seek the face of God that He might bestow upon us of his eternal holiness, for to those who yield themselves to Him He has promised everlasting peace and rest.

We realised that the chaplain was in earnest and believed himself every word he spoke, and we all knew that there would be a fight and that perhaps we were going to suffer a sudden death or painful wounds and sorrowful transport. And then there faced us all the hard, long, weary road through shocking diseases and gnawing hunger and torturing thirst before we came again to our distant native land. Therefore, we all listened with great seriousness and then took off our hats for the prayer.

At ten o'clock we got started. The country was rolling and covered with thin bush. We went along the top of a low ridge and saw in the moonlight the beautiful soft lines of the hills; below in the low ground ran a broad bright stripe, the sandy bed of a river. It got to be four o'clock, then morning, and nothing was to be seen of the enemy.

We thought, however, that we should see them when we reached the height in front of us, and in spite of the ever-increasing heat we went on. The van reached the height and disappeared. Not a shot. We saw that the artillery were taking the dust caps off their guns. A few shots were heard from a long way ahead. Now we reached the top. Nothing was to be seen of the enemy except below in the distance, where a heavy, monstrous cloud of dust was moving swiftly across the plain. Then it was clear that the proud nation had lost all courage and hope, and preferred to die in the desert rather than to fight any more with us.

We rested a little by the water-holes which the enemy had left, and by their fires, which were still burning. Then, on weary horses, we pushed forward. Towards evening, as we passed along by the river bed, we came to a place where there should have been water. We found some old water-holes, and near them hundreds of new ones dug by the enemy the day before. They were twelve feet deep and even deeper, but they had no water in them.

It was now reported that there was still a last water-place about five hours' ride further on, and that great numbers of the enemy were camping there. It was decided that we must drive them away; and we wanted to, for if we hunted them out of that place nothing remained to them but the wilderness. At one o'clock at night, tired riders and weary horses, we formed for the march. In seven hours we reached the place, but no water was there. From a hill, we saw two mighty clouds of dust moving rapidly to the north and northeast, toward certain death from thirst.

But we, too, had reached our limit. Every fourth man was sick with dysentery or typhoid fever; the rest were exhausted from overexertion. Half our horses had fallen, our clothes and saddles were torn. We were seven hours from the nearest, poorly supplied water-holes and twenty-four hours from the better ones. The danger of getting hung up here on the border of the desert was not remote. Then the general ordered that we should give up the pursuit.

Still some scouts were to try to push on for a few hours more. Volunteers in plenty offered themselves even for this last hard expedition, as they always did for all scouting trips. As I was a good rider, I got the horse of a non-commissioned officer who had just slipped sick out of his saddle, and I rode out of camp with the party. A first lieutenant who looked like a scholar led us. We rode and rode; then we rested an hour. When we had trotted painfully for ten minutes, we dismounted and led our horses, and we even resorted to having one man lead two horses while the other drove them along from behind. So, we got on comparatively fast. The lieutenant's voice was hoarse in his dry throat from commanding: "Dismount!" "Mount!" "Trot!"

Several times we saw from some little elevation the mass of dust which dragged slowly forward, but we got little nearer. We thought they would have to rest; then we would come up to them with a last effort and frighten them by our sudden appearance and firing, and drive them still further into the desert. The sun was burning fiercely on the broad, desert country. My throat was so parched that every time I followed the impulse to swallow, I groaned softly with the pain. I had sometimes a sudden feeling of fear that I must get away out of this terribly dry, hot air and scorching sun or I should all at once, with one fearful scream, lose my reason. I could not refrain from drinking my last drop of water and moistening my eyes with the damp sack.

Soon after this, one of our twenty men began to sway in his saddle and to murmur to himself. When I looked back to see how it was with the others, two or three were hanging pale and insensible in their saddles and others rode along with deep-sunken, closed eyes. The subordinate officer looked at me with a glance which seemed to say: "It is madness to ride any farther." Immediately afterwards the lieutenant called a halt and had five men dismount and lie down. We protected them from the heat with their cloaks and rode on. But after about an hour five or six of the party could no longer lead their horses; their legs were like lead, and two were trembling in every limb and vomiting. We let them lie down and covered them up. They were hardly on the ground before they were sleeping like the dead.

I noticed that the lieutenant was annoyed that he could not go on, although he himself could hardly speak. He stood and looked with the glass up the hill behind which the cloud of dust had vanished, hanging now only like a mist over the summit. He wanted very much for us to show ourselves on the top, in case the enemy had halted on the other side in the hope that the German troops had at last turned back. A home-guardsman who was in the party stepped up to him and said that his horse was probably strong enough to ride on two hours more, especially as it was getting toward evening.

Then I, too, stepped forward and offered to ride with them. We arranged with the others that they should go back to the first five and wait there with them till ten o'clock. If we had not then returned, they were to avail themselves of the remaining night hours to reach the camp. I had a secret opinion that the two would not give up their plan till they collapsed from over-exhaustion, and I wanted to be with them, for I thought I was stronger than either of them.

After half an hour, we started. We gave up leading our horses and stayed in the saddle. After a while three cows came toward us. They were awfully thin and lowed mournfully; one of them had been cut in the side with a knife, probably so that someone could drink the blood that flowed out. A little further on we found a goat lying by the way, and near it a boy with remarkably long, thin legs, as if they had stretched in death. We hardly turned our horses so that they should not tread on him. It is strange what a matter of indifference another man's life is to us when he belongs to another race.

In half an hour or more we neared the height. The guardsman rode on ahead, his gun in his hand. The lieutenant and I followed. It was slow work. As I was peering by chance into some bushes about fifty yards off, which grew thicker together than the others, I saw among and under them people sitting in crowds, shoulder against shoulder, quite motionless. The heads of some drooped on their breasts and their arms hung down, as if they were asleep. Others sat leaning against a bush or a neighbour, breathing fast and hard, their mouths open; they regarded us with stupid eyes. Some, women and children, had laid themselves down across the legs and laps of those who were sitting. I quietly told my companions what I saw. They cast a long glance in the direction which I indicated, but said nothing.

We rode on. The guardsman pointed once or twice into the bushes; I looked over there. Thus, we reached the summit and then looked attentively out over the plain, which lay in boundless extent and absolute stillness, like a yellowish grey sea. The long rays of the setting sun lay upon it like strips of thin, bright-shining cloth.

We sprang off our horses, loosened the girths, and lay down on the ground. The guard's horse began to sniff at his face, but he did not notice it; he was already asleep. The lieutenant stood up again and said to me: "Get up! If we fall asleep, we shall sleep all night and then we are lost." I rose, and we both stood awhile with benumbed senses in a state between sleeping and waking. The sun sank in a dull glow; the air grew cooler, and the horses got somewhat more lively and began with weary steps to nibble a few little bushes.

After a while the Africander woke and asked in a woe-begone voice if I had a drop of water.

I said: "No."

He said: "The lieutenant has some, then."

Again, I said: "No."

Then he said he could hold out no longer without water,—he had trusted too much to his strength, he should have to die here. The lieutenant, who had dozed standing by his horse and holding on to the saddle, woke and said consolingly: "Cheer up! We shall start at once. Then we are off for home, for the war is now really over."

"Yes," said the guardsman, "it is over; forty thousand of them are dead; all their land belongs to us. But what good does all that do me? I must die here." He begged mournfully: "Have you not a single drop of water?"

The lieutenant shook his head: "You know I have none. Rest a little longer; it is night, and that will refresh us."

The guardsman got up with difficulty and went with bent back down the slope to one side where there were some bushes. I said: "What does he want? I believe he is out of his senses and wants to search for water." At that moment, there came from the bushes into which he had vanished a noise of cursing, running, and leaping. Immediately he reappeared, holding by the hip a tall, thin negro dressed in European clothing. He tore the negro's gun from his hand and, swearing at him in a strange language, dragged him up to us and said: "The wretch has a German gun, but no more cartridges."

The guardsman had now become quite lively, and began to talk to his captive, threatening him and kicking him in the knees. The negro crouched, and answered every question with a great flow of words and with quick, very agile and remarkable gestures of the arms and hands. "He says he has not taken part in the war." Then he asked him some more questions, pointing towards the east; and the negro also pointed towards the east, answering all sorts of things of which I understood nothing. The guardsman said: "He is stuffing me with lies."

This went on for some time. I can still hear the two dry, shrill voices of the German and the native. Apparently, the guardsman at last learned enough, for he said: "The missionary said to me, 'Beloved, don't forget that the blacks are our brothers.' Now I will give my brother his reward." He pushed the black man off and said: "Run away!"

The man sprang up and tried to get down across the clearing in long zigzag jumps, but be had not taken five leaps before the ball hit him and he pitched forward at full length and lay still.

I grumbled a little; I thought the shot might attract to us the attention of hostile tribes who had perhaps stayed behind. But the lieutenant thought I meant it was not right for the guardsman to shoot the negro, and said in his thoughtful, scholarly way: "Safe is safe. He can't raise a gun against as any more, nor beget any more children to fight against us. The struggle for South Africa will still be a hard one, whether it is to belong to the Germans or to the blacks."

The guardsman was leaning against his horse. He had a severe pain in his chest, and in a distressed voice said:

"When we were sitting once by our fire there in the south, our captain said that two million Germans would live here, and their children would ride safely through the country and visit their playmates, stopping on the way to water their horses at these water-holes and at many new ones which would be dug everywhere. But I shall not see anything of it; I am sick, very sick. Haven't you a single drop of water?"

He supported himself by the saddle and looked out with fixed eyes over the *steppes*, above which the stars were shining.

The lieutenant talked to him, prevailed upon him to lie down, and covered him up with his cloak. He himself stood by his horse, beating time with his watch, which he held in his hand, in order to keep himself awake. So, we both stood for a good while. Then he spoke:

"These blacks have deserved death before God and man, not because they have murdered two hundred farmers and have revolted against us, but because they have built no houses and dug no wells."

Then he fell to talking about home, and among other things said:

"What we sang the day before yesterday in the service, 'We come to pray before God the just,' I understood in this way: God has let us conquer here because we are the nobler and more advanced people. That is not saying much in comparison with this black nation, but we must see to it that we become better and braver before all nations of the earth. To the nobler and more vigorous belongs the world. That is the justice of God."

The guardsman had gone to sleep. The lieutenant stood erect, his watch in his hand, swaying a little from time to time. I stood half asleep and half-awake by the side of my horse. The moon rose and the night grew cold and windy. After a while the lieutenant spoke again: "But the missionary was right when he said that all men are brothers."

"Then we have killed our brother," said I, looking toward the dark body lying stretched in the grass.

He looked up and said in a hoarse, painful voice:

"For a long time, we must be hard and kill, but at the same time as individual men we must strive toward high thoughts and noble deeds so that we may contribute our part to mankind, our future brothers."

He gazed thoughtfully over the broad plain and looked again at the motionless body.

After a while the lieutenant signified with a motion of the hand that we should break our rest. He went with heavy steps to the sleeping man, woke him, and with difficulty set him on his feet, and ordered me to pull up the girths. Then we helped the guardsman into the saddle, mounted ourselves, and rode away.

Those whom we had left behind we found in a dead sleep; the subordinate officer, on a saddle in their midst, alone sat watching. It was a tiresome ride the rest of the night. Some were continually begging for water; two had to be supported in their saddles. I myself know little of those hours; my spirit was far away sleeping and dreaming. An hour after sunrise, when the heat was beginning to be oppressive, we reached the main body. They were preparing to break camp. The campaign was over.

CHAPTER 17

Last Days in Africa

So, we set forth out of the far east and marched westward toward the capital. Many more than half of us had to go on foot with packs over our shoulders.

It was in the month of October, the time when in that region spring is advancing over the land. Rain and thunder-storms had passed violently over the plain and were still occurring. So new life was beginning to shoot up out of the earth that had looked so un-fruitful. Flowers appeared in the long, yellowish grass and filled the air with their sweet, mild perfume. The loathed thorn-bush put on dark green leaves and snow-white blossoms. Many of us went up and plucked a gay branch from the hated plant. The single, tall trees decked themselves out with long-stemmed yellow or lilac umbels; others had feathery flowers of snowy whiteness. And high, high above all the fresh green and the glorious pure white and the rich yellow, arched the cloudless blue sky. If we had been really well and had had enough to eat and had not had to pass the columns of sick transports and the new graves, it would have been indeed a beautiful journey.

I had long liked the strange country, yet I did not want to stay in it; I would not give up my parents and my trade. Still, my mind was firmly made up to visit it again in after years, and I shall do so. There were not a few among us who liked the country better and better the more they learned to know it, and who seriously intended to stay and become farmers. If even a half of those carried out their intention, about five hundred of us would remain in the country.

When we were still ten days' march from the capital and were sit-ting comfortably around our fire with better food—for a provision wagon had arrived with bacon and coffee and other good things—and were talking again about our joyous home-going! Henry Gehlsen came over to us from headquarters and told us that the Hottentots, who lived in the south, had risen, and that now a second campaign would begin which would probably be as hard as the one which had just ended; at any rate, going home was not to be thought of.

At that we became very still Then we gave vent to our amazement and began to rail. A Berlin soldier who was sitting with us came finally to a conclusion, saying: "Well, it is all the same to me, but my mother will scold." We discussed the matter for a long time and went to other mess companies, where we asked all sorts of questions and learned all sorts of things. Late in the evening a violent thunderstorm rose in the south till it reached the broad, dry river bed; flickering flashes of lightning filled the whole southern sky till after midnight. It was as if to let us know how severe the struggle would be which was in prospect down there. Towards morning the night got bitter cold and windy.

The following morning the lieutenant with whom I had made the last scouting expedition asked me if I would escort him as fast as possible to the capital; he was sick, and did not want to break down on the road. I was only too ready, and rode with him as fast as our horses could go. On the third or fourth day, it struck me that my heart was beating very loud and hard. I often pressed my hand against it and said, "What is the matter with you? Be quiet!" but it did no good. Nor did I think much of it when on the fourth or fifth day I fainted for the first time in my life. I had, too, plenty to do in holding the lieutenant on his saddle, for he had summoned the last remnant of his strength to finish this ride.

When on the morning of the eighth day we were riding through the capital, the stabbing pain in my heart became unendurable. I managed to escort the lieutenant to the door of the hospital and then to ride at a walk up to the fort. But there I was lifted fainting from my horse by fellow-soldiers who came running up. They carried me into the hospital, where the doctor examined me. He said that I had contracted a weakness of the heart from long overstraining and especially from this last hard ride, and that I could not now live in a country with such a high altitude and such thin air; I must go home.

So after I had lain for a week in the hospital, I travelled by the little rattling railroad to the coast in four uncomfortable day-journeys in the small open beet cars; and on the second day after my arrival there, I clambered in my guardsman's uniform with knapsack and cloak up the rope-ladder to the deck of the Wörmann steamer.

We were fifty men on board, most of us sick, some very sick. One had received a wound in the breast, and it was still suppurating. We often sat by him and carried him on his cot out into the sun and tried to comfort him. But he had no courage, and would lie brooding and sometimes softly crying. I do not know what became of him. Another, a day labourer's son from Pomerania, had lost a leg; he could already hobble about on crutches and he acted as if he were in good spirits. He said he could now sing the song which they often used to sing in the village school: "For all I am and have, I thank thee, my Fatherland."

But he frequently sat with a grave face in his long chair; he was only twenty-three years old. Still another had been sunstruck on a forced march and had ever since had fixed notions which grew worse all the time during the journey. He thought he was the king of South Africa, and wanted to order cannon in Germany. I have heard that afterwards he entirely recovered. The rest were almost all suffering from heart disease or had undergone a bad case of typhoid fever. We were all friendly with one another and agreed very well. There was only one, a Berliner, who became more unpopular every day; he had and knew and could do everything.

I had saved up one hundred and fifty *marks* from my war bounty, and I spent it in purchase of a second-cabin passage. Henry Gehlsen, who had got through a bad case of typhoid fever and was also going home, had suggested it to me. I was glad to do it, and have never regretted it. Whoever keeps up a respectable outward appearance will by that very means be helped to succeed better in everything else, too. I associated mostly with Gehlsen and a gunner in the navy, whose duty it was to serve the armor-plated turret on a man-of-war. He had been with Gehlsen and me in our first bad fight. He was a broad-shouldered, genial man, full of jokes and drollery.

I liked him especially because he gave the benefit of his continual and great humour not only to the well but particularly to the invalid fellows. Although almost all had some sort of injury, we were nevertheless all joyful over our return. As far as to the coast of Spain the deck witnessed much joking, singing, and nonsense. I myself could contribute nothing to it, but I enjoyed it all very much. We were exceedingly happy when we saw the coast of England again. Just after that we met the first German ship, a little slender cruiser of our navy, still quite new. It steamed energetically by. At evening the next day, a Wörmann steamer came toward us which had on board troops for the campaign against the Hottentots. They stood by the rail in their big grey cloaks and soft hats, and shouted across to us.

The next evening, about five o'clock, we neared Cuxhaven; we plainly saw it lying in the twilight. Although the weather was biting cold, we stood at the rail for a long time, wrapped in our thick coats. Only when it was quite dark did we go below. About one o'clock at night we made fast to the Petersen quay at Hamburg, but we stayed on board overnight.

In the forenoon, the physician came and looked every one of us over. Then the very sick men went ashore; then we. I went with permission into the city to visit my uncle who lives in St. Pauli. I was to travel in the afternoon to Kiel to report myself and get my dismissal.

When I was sauntering along the *Jungfernstieg* in my worn-out, dirty cord uniform, with dark, sunburned face, a middle-aged man came up and joined me, and asked me all sorts of questions as we went along. In the course of the conversation it came out that I had heard of him in my father's house; for he had known my father from childhood. I related to him all that I had seen and experienced, and what I had thought of it all. And he has made this book out of it.

German South West Africa
By Francis J. Reynolds

REBELLION IN UNION OF SOUTH AFRICA

German South West Africa, in 1914, was in a different situation at the outbreak of the war from that of the German colonies of the east and west. Over the frontier was a self-governing dominion, the Union of South Africa, with an independent parliament made up of a strange mixture of different parties. The irreconcilables in the Dutch population who had dreamed of a greater Afrikander Republic, would they not take this opportunity to side with Germany who promised to further their ambitions? Great Britain expected some trouble from this element in the Union, and prepared for the worst, while Germany was equally active, and there was much intriguing to persuade the Dutch to cast in their lot with them. In other parts of Africa, Germany had to fight hear battles unaided, but here in the enemy's camp there was every hope of gaining powerful assistance. Until the situation in the Union became clear, it was Germany's part to defend her colony in South West Africa, hoping by a brave display of arms to win over the Dutch, who were bitter against England.

German South West Africa enjoys many natural advantages. Her capital is far in the interior. Between her railway on the south, which almost reaches the Cape frontier, and her border spreads out the desert of Kalahari and the arid, waterless plains of northwest Cape Colony. The branch railways are separated by about 200 miles from German territory, and on the northern line Kimberley was a little less than 400 miles distant. British forces entering the colony by land must encounter many difficulties, especially in the desert region, which the Germans left undefended. because they believed it could not be crossed by troops.

Before the war, according to the official returns, the colony had a force of 3,500 men, mainly whites; but with reserves and volunteers from among the population of German blood it has been variously estimated that an army of from 6,000 to 10,000 men could be gathered together. The Germans were believed to be strong in artillery, and were known to have sixty-six batteries of Maxims. There was also a camel corps 500 strong.

After the declaration of war in August, 1914, Dr. Seitz, the German Governor, began to carry out his plan of defence. In the second week of August, 1914, the Germans abandoned Swakopmund and Lüderitz Bay, their principal stations on the coast, and after destroying the jetty and tugs in harbour, retired with their military stores to Windhoek, the inland capital. In the last weeks in August they made short dashes into British territory, entrenching themselves in some places, and occasionally engaged in a skirmish with farmers on the frontier.

Thus, when the Union Parliament met September 8, 1914, it was informed by General Botha, the Premier, that Germany had begun hostilities against the British colonies. On the following day, as a challenge to the pro-German party, he moved a resolution to convey to King George an address, assuring him of the loyal support of the Union. Upon this General Hertzog moved an amendment to the effect that attacking German territory in South Africa was against the interests of the Union and the empire. But the victory was with General Botha's Government when the questions were voted on. Only 12 of the 104 votes cast were in favour of Hertzog's amendment.

It was evident that many *burghers* living in districts on the borders of German South West Africa shared Hertzog's opinion, and were opposed to taking offensive measures against the German colony as long as the Union was left in peace. From the time that Hertzog had been dropped from Botha's cabinet he had posed as a martyr. His adherents believed that he had been "sacrificed to please the English," and that Botha was merely a tool in the hands of the British Government.

The spirit of rebellion in the Union did not show itself openly for some time, but the leaders—Beyers, De Wet, Maritz, and Kemp— were busy conspiring and stirring up disaffection among the *burghers* who had never become reconciled to the Union.

De Wet, because of his world-wide fame during the Boer War, has been given undue prominence for the part he played in the rebellion. He was not the head and front of the movement, though his name was one to conjure with among the disaffected Boers, and he proved to be a valuable recruiting agent. His operations during the rebellion, as will be subsequently shown, were generally ineffective in the field, and terminated ingloriously, before he could work any great harm.

General Beyers, the most dangerous foe the Union had in the rebellion, was a direct contrast to the rude and unlettered De Wet. He was young and brave, and had shown himself one of the ablest soldiers the British had to fight against during the Boer War. He looked the dashing officer that he was—tall, straight, black bearded, and with his pleasant manners and easy speech, he was just the man to inspire enthusiasm in others.

Colonel Maritz and Colonel Kemp, the other chief leaders in the rebellion, had never been as prominent in South African affairs as Beyers and De Wet. Maritz had shown ability as a leader in the Boer War, had held various military positions since, and at the beginning of the European War was in command of the South African border between the Union and German South West Africa, to which he had been appointed by Beyers, who was commandant general of the citizen forces. General Smuts, the Minister of Defence, may have suspected some sinister motives in this appointment, for Maritz had many friends in the German colony, but for the present he had to keep his suspicions to himself and await some overt act of offense.

Colonel Kemp, the remaining chief leader, had never done anything to give him special prominence. He had proved himself an efficient soldier during the Boer War, and appears to have been in command of a training camp in the western Transvaal when the rebellion was started.

Under these four leaders, acting independently, or in conjunction with them, were subleaders, an indefinite number, members of the Government, and men connected with the church and army, whose part in the rebellion was to stir up the people.

An interesting character among the somewhat nebulous subleaders in the rebellion was Van Rensburg, sometimes called "Prophet" Lichtenberg, from the place where he lived. During the Boer War, he had predicted a remarkable victory for the Boers, which had resulted in the capture of Lord Methuen, and ever since the *burghers* of the Union had held him in reverential awe. When the war with Germany broke out he made various prophecies. He discovered that the events foretold in the Book of Revelations would now take place. Germany, he said, had been divinely ordained to conquer the world and purify it. Any attempt to resist this divine ordinance would be punished by the righteous anger of an offended deity. Nor was the "prophet" forgetful of local politics, for he had another "vision" in which he predicted that Generals Delarey, Beyers, and De Wet were divinely appointed leaders, who would restore the old republic. These "prophecies" were spread broadcast throughout the Union, were eagerly believed by the superstitious *burghers*, and served to hearten up the disaffected who had some grudge against the Government.

A great meeting of the *burghers* was summoned to meet August 15, 1914, at Treurfontein. This date had been fixed because Van Rensburg in a "vision" had seen "a dark cloud, with blood flowing from it, inscribed with number 15, and General Delarey, the uncrowned king of western Transvaal, returning home without his hat, followed by a carriage full of flowers." Eight hundred *burghers* attended the meeting, but Delarey, who spoke, had been warned by General Botha, and therefore spoke calmly, urging the *burghers* to remain cool and await events. Such was Delarey's influence over the assembly, who had come expecting to make a fiery speech, that a resolution expressing confidence in the Government was passed.

On September 15, 1914, General Christian Beyers resigned his position of *commandant* general of the defence force in a letter which was practically a declaration of war against the British Empire. It developed that for some weeks he had been organising rebellion. He was secretly arranging a scheme of operations in which the German forces were to take part, while making plans for the Union Government. He hoped to win over General Delarey, leader of the Boers in the western Transvaal, but this officer was accidentally killed by the police near Johannesburg. The patrol out looking for the notorious Jackson gang of bandits, then in the neighbourhood, had orders to examine any motorcar and fire at once, if when summoned to stop their challenge was ignored. The car bearing Generals Beyers and Delarey had been twice challenged while passing through the town. The third time a policeman fired at the wheel to disable the car, and the bullet ricocheted and killed Delarey.

A thousand armed Boers at this time were encamped at Potchefstroom in Delarey's district. Colonel Kemp, who had sent in his resignation to the Union Government, and was working here for Delarey, had won over their officers, and on parade urged the men to refuse to volunteer for German South West Africa. He also collected in his tent such ammunition as he could lay his hands upon.

The death of General Delarey disconcerted General Beyers, and his fellow conspirators, and Colonel Kemp withdrew his resignation from the Union army. Over the grave of Delarey General Beyers, in the presence of General Botha, declared that he had no intention of advising or causing a rebellion, yet the following day, with General De Wet and others, he was urging the Boers who had come to the funeral of their dead leader to revolt against active service should the commandos be called out under the Defence Act.

Botha knew the men who were stirring up rebellion and acted quickly. He called for volunteers, announcing that he would lead in person the Union forces against the Germans, and the immediate response he received was gratifying. The conspirators remained quiet for some weeks, but General Beyers and De Wet were secretly at work against the Government of the Union.

On September 26, 1914, Colonel Grant and a small force of African Rifles and Transvaal Horse Artillery operating at Sandfontein near the German border were trapped by two German battalions while on their way to a water hole. From the heights, the German guns swept the circular basin below where the Union force was gathered. The advantage was all in favour of the Germans. High explosive shells from ten guns wrought havoc among the South African soldiers, but not until their ammunition ran out and every man of their gun crews was either killed or wounded would the little band of Boers and Britons surrender. It developed later that Lieutenant Colonel S. G. Maritz, a Boer leader commanding Union forces in the Northwest territory, had turned traitor and arranged the disaster. It was through General Beyers that he had been appointed to an important command on the German border.

Maritz who was now ordered by General Smuts, Minister of Defence, to report to headquarters and give up his command, sent a defiant reply October 8, 1914. He stated that in addition to his own troops he had German guns and men, and had signed an agreement with the Governor of South West Africa ceding Walfish Bay (a British possession) and certain portions of Union territory in return for a guarantee of the independence of the South African Republic. All his officers and men who were unwilling to join him had been sent as prisoners into German territory.

General Botha replied to the rebel by proclaiming martial law throughout the Union. General Brits, with the Imperial Light Horse, was sent to capture Maritz, and in an engagement October 15, 1914, at Ratedraii, near Uppington, took seventy rebel prisoners.

On October 22, 1914, Maritz with 1000 rebels and seventy German gunners, attacked at dawn the post of Keimos, where there were only 150 loyalists. The little garrison held out until out until re-enforcements arrived and the battle then turned against Maritz, who offered to surrender for a free pardon. This being refused, the fight went on, and Maritz eventually fled wounded into German territory. Two days later a party of rebels with German gunners were defeated at Kakamas.

General Hertzog, who had represented the pro-German party in the Union Parliament, gathered a commando and broke out in revolt on October 21, 1914; He issued a manifesto complaining of English oppression, and announced that he would tolerate it no longer: Three members of the Union Parliament and a member of the Defence Council, Mr. Wessel-Wessels, came out in arms. In the Western Transvaal and the northern Free State, the rebel leaders had about 10,000 men in separate groups. Their plan was to join their commandos with a force under Maritz from German South West Africa.

The situation from a military point of view seemed to be serious for the Union, but Generals Botha and Smuts were active and resourceful and in a few weeks had 40,000 men in the field. The loyal Boers were in a difficult position, for now they were asked to fight against their own kith and kin for the British Empire. In battle, the Dutch generals showed that they were anxious to spare their own kinsmen, and ordered their men to withhold firing, to the last moment, hoping that the rebels would surrender. The rebels were not allowed time to join their forces, for General Botha, gave them no rest night or day.

On October 27, 1914, General Beyers and his commando operating near Rustenburg were driven in headlong flight all day long by General Botha and a force of loyalists. Two days later General Beyers was a fugitive. His scattered commandos were defeated by Colonel Alberts at Lichtenburg and again at Zuitpansdrift on November 5, 1914. Meanwhile, Colonel Kemp, who had been acting with General Beyers, now separated from his chief, and with a large force started for German South West Africa, pursued by Colonel Alberts. Beyers, trying to get in touch with De Wet, entered the Orange Free State, closely followed by a large loyalist force under Colonel Lemmer.

On November 7, 1914, Beyers's commando was attacked by Lemmer near the Vet River and though Beyers led in person, he was defeated, and, 864 of his men being captured and about 20 killed or wounded, the fugitive remnant returned to Hoopstad. De Wet, whom

General Beyers had been prevented from joining by the activity of the loyalist forces, had gathered together in the northern districts of the Orange Free State a poorly organized body of soldiers, but sufficient in numbers to cause the South African Government some anxiety. Negotiations between the Free State leaders and De Wet postponed for a time any military action by the Government, but the old guerrilla captain was not to be pacified. There had been a rivalry between him and Botha in the Boer war, and he seemed anxious to measure strength now with a soldier whom he considered his inferior.

De Wet's name was a power in the land, especially among the "poor whites" and the squatter class, who without much intelligence or education had not prospered under new conditions in the Union. They were without hope for the future and felt that they were being crowded out by the more active spirits in the country. They saw in the rebellion a chance to improve their economic position. There was little to lose and much might be won. A new Afrikander Republic would bring back the old days for which they had never ceased to long for. It was from this class of malcontents that De Wet drew the bulk of his men. The rest were religious fanatics, disgruntled politicians, wastrels and adventurers.

We have said previously that De Wet's recruits were poorly organised. It was a weakness of this brilliant guerrilla fighter that he could not maintain discipline when handling a large body of men, and the sort of troops he was working with in the rebellion called for the sternest kind of authority to make them effective soldiers. He only enjoyed a month of freedom and covered considerable territory, but he accomplished very little from a military point of view. He could not follow the same tactics that he had employed in the Boer war with equal success now. At home on the back of a horse, it was impossible for him to slip through the enemy's lines as of old when there were motor cars to pursue. He began his campaign with an action at Winburg where he defeated a small loyalist commando under Cronje, and where one of his sons was killed.

A battle of considerable importance was fought on November 12, 1914, at Marquard to the east of Winburg. General Botha and his Transvaal commando by a forced night march had reached Winburg the day before and getting in touch with De Wet's forces encircled them on the east and northeast. Colonel Brandt at the same time led his commando from Winburg within easy reach of De Wet, while General Lukin, and Colonel Brits moving forward from the west completed the hemming in of the enemy. General Botha's commando attacked De Wet's forces and defeated them with great loss. If General Lukin and Colonel Brits had not been delayed in taking up their positions all the rebels would have been captured. The victory was especially of far-reaching importance because it discouraged De Wet's hopes and strengthened the loyalist cause. All of De Wet's stores of food and ammunition were taken, and a hundred carts, wagons and motor cars, while the prisoners numbered about 250.

De Wet, with a Boer commando in pursuit now fled up the Vet River, then turning south at Boshoff, divided his decreasing force into two divisions. Leading one of these he turned again north, reaching the Vaal River with only 25 men remaining of the 2,000 he had fought with at Marquard.

Beaten back by a loyal outpost he succeeded in crossing the Vaal on November 21, 1914, closely pursued by Commandant Dutoit and a motor car contingent from Witwatersrand. De Wet's followers had gradually deserted, and he had only four men with him when he succeeded in joining a small commando of fugitives gathered at Schweizer Renek. The heavy rainstorms at this time favoured him as he started with this force to follow Colonel Kemp and join Maritz in German South West Africa, for the motorcars in pursuit could make small progress over the heavy roads. Crossing Bechuanaland on November 25, 1914, De Wet was pursued by another loyalist force under Colonel Brits who in two days captured half of the fugitives.

On December 1, 1914, at a farm at Waterburg, about a hundred miles from Mafeking, De Wet and his party of 52 men surrendered to Colonel Jordaan without firing a shot, and the one-time Commander in Chief of the Orange Free State forces was imprisoned at Johannesburg to await his trial for high treason.

In the Orange Free State, General Beyers and about seventy men harried by loyal commandos divided his party, and leading one group made a dash for the Vaal River pursued by Captain Uys and Cornet Deneker with a small force. Trapped at daybreak on December 9, 1914, near the Vaal, Beyers and a few men tried to swim the river to the Transvaal under a fierce fire. Beyers was seen to fall from his horse, and was heard to cry for help, but was drowned before anyone could come to the rescue.

General Botha's operations in the northern district of the Orange Free State were made difficult because of the heavy fogs, but early in December, 1914, the rebels were in sore straits, 500 being captured while 200 surrendered to Commandant Kloppers a loyalist, who had been taken a prisoner and was afterwards released.

General Maritz, Colonel Kemp, and the "Prophet" Litchtenburg had fled west, and after some fighting at Kurumun, and two minor successes, surprising two posts at Langklip and Onydas which they were forced to abandon on the arrival of re-enforcements, they retired toward the German frontier where they were penned in by the Union forces.

On January 24, 1915, the rebels made their last sally, attacking Colonel Van der Venter at Upington. The rebel force, about 1,200 strong and led by Maritz and Kemp, was easily repulsed. On February 3, 1915, Maritz, having fled to German territory, Colonel Kemp and his commando of 43 officers. and 486 men including the "Prophet Lichtenburg surrendered.

INVASION OF GERMAN SOUTH WEST AFRICA

Within the first six months of the war the rebellion had been crushed. One reason for its speedy decline and fall was the general amnesty offered to all rebels who surrendered voluntarily by November 21, 1914. But to General Botha and his lieutenant, General Smuts, credit must be given for their masterly operations in the field, and the clear-headed way in which the campaign against the rebels was conducted. In less than two months General Botha had harried them from all points of the compass until they lost their nerve and became at last dispirited and weary.

In numbers, they were sufficient to prolong the conflict for a much longer period, but the quick moves made by Botha's men made it impossible for them to concentrate at any given point. Separated from each other in isolated bands it was impossible even with the best fighting to gain a notable victory. During the campaign, General Botha had taken 7,000 prisoners, while the total casualty list of the Union Army was only 334. In the hour of triumph, he showed great magnanimity. The rank and file of the rebel army were not punished, but members of the defence force who had violated their military oath were placed on trial for their life.

Now that the rebellion at home had been disposed of, General Botha could turn his attention to his long-projected invasion of German South West Africa. As originally planned the expedition was weak in numbers, inadequately trained, was without aircraft, and lacked sufficient artillery, but all these deficiencies were now made good.

On January 5, 1915, the *burgher* force reassembled, and began to encamp on Green Point Common on the way to German South West Africa. Thousands of Boers, freshly trained for war through their recent operations against the rebels, were with this army of invasion.

German South West Africa was in some respects one of the most valuable of Germany's colonial possessions in Africa. It contains 320,000 square miles, which is about the size of Germany and Italy together. It has a seacoast of 800 miles on the west, is bordered on the north by the Portuguese colony of Angola, and on the east by the British Protectorate of Bechuanaland. Its shortest frontier of all is the Cape of Good Hope on the south. The population numbers about 100,000 natives and 15,000 German settlers.

There are two ports on the coast; Lüderitz Bay and Swakopmund. Near the latter is the little British enclave of Walfish Bay, used as a trading and whaling station. Diamond mines were discovered near Lüderitz Bay in 1906, and copper is also found in the country. There are some hundreds of miles of bleak and sandy desert which presented many difficulties to the Union forces invading the country.

The British Government attained great importance to the conquest of German South West Africa and offered a loan of £7,000,000 for the expenses of the campaign.

General Botha planned an enveloping movement against Windhoek, the capital, about 200 miles from the coast. He divided his forces into two armies, the northern under his command to use Swakopmund as a base and to follow the railway to Windhoek. The army of the south under General Smuts was divided into three separate columns. One under Sir Duncan Mackenzie was to move East along the railway from Lüderitz Bay. Another under Colonel Berrange was to invade the colony from the east, and a third column commanded by Colonel Van der Venter was to march north along the line running down Warmbad to Keetmanshoop. Botha's plans, if successful, would drive the German forces away from modern communications into a waterless desert region, from which they could not easily escape.

The two German ports were occupied, and at the beginning of February, 1916, the four principal gates into the colony were in Union hands.

British Conquest of South West Africa

Our attention is now drawn to South West Africa. In the first week of February, 1915, the Germans made a determined effort to break through the encircling armies that were closing in on them. Kakamas on the Orange, where a British garrison was stationed to protect Schuit Drift, was fiercely attacked on February 5 by about 600 Germans, well equipped with Maxims and machine guns. They were beaten off after a short engagement with a loss of nine men killed, twenty-two wounded, and fifteen taken prisoners. On the Union side, the casualties were one killed, and two wounded.

On February 22, 1915, General Botha's army being ready, he moved out of Swakopmund, and on the following day occupied the stations of Nonidas and Goanikontes, meeting with only slight resistance. Nearly a month was now spent in preparing for the advance on the capital, Windhoek. Careful reconnoitring of the enemy's positions was made, and an advanced base was established.

On the night of March 19, 1915, two mounted brigades left the post at Husab to clear the railway line. General Botha accompanied the first brigade, which was commanded by Colonel Brits, their object being Riet, an important place south of the railway, where it was known that the enemy was strongly prepared. Riet was of utmost importance to the Union force for it commanded the highway to Windhoek. It was planned that while Colonel Brits's brigade attacked Riet the Bloemhof Commando was to execute a flank movement and seizing Schwarze Kopje to endeavour to cut off the enemy's retreat.

At daybreak on March 20, 1915, the brigade reached the German position. The right rested on the Swakop stream; the left on the foothills of Langer Heinrichberg, while the artillery was effectively placed so as to command the river and highway. Assisted by the guns of the Transvaal Horse Artillery a frontal attack was made, and the fighting became general. With varying fortunes, it continued until the evening when the Germans were finally driven out and dispersed.

The second brigade commanded by Colonel Celliers had been directed to cut the railway line between Jakalswater and Sphinx. He was to attack the former place after blocking the way, in case any reenforcements should be sent by the enemy from Windhoek. Celliers succeeded in cutting the railway and seized a train containing supplies for the Germans, but his attack on Jakalswater was a failure, and the enemy made forty-three of his men prisoners.

General Botha was so confident of the ultimate success of his campaign, that he was not disposed to imperil his chances by any hasty operations, and so his progress toward Windhoek was at first necessarily slow. The nature of the country afforded the enemy many natural advantages and unfortunately the Union forces were not provided with aeroplanes, which would have proved invaluable in scouting.

Pforto, a station on the line where the Germans occupied a strong position, was surrounded by a column led by Colonel Alberts. The enemy had two large guns and a number of Maxims. A charge by the Union force and the effective work of their battery soon silenced the enemy's artillery. The Germans had lost twenty killed, of whom three were officers, when they surrendered unconditionally. There were 210 prisoners taken, four guns and a large quantity of ammunition.

General Botha was engaged in April and May, 1915, clearing the railway system of the enemy. To prevent any flank attacks, it was necessary to hold the two main lines, which run from Swakopmund north to Grootfontein, Tsumeb, and to Windhoek. This line being cleared for fifty miles, Colonel Skinner and the Kimberley Regiment were stationed at Trekopje, which became the Union railhead.

On April 26, 1915, about 700 Germans and a dozen guns vigorously assailed this encampment and for four hours the fight raged with varying consequences. The Germans under a withering fire from their batteries tried to surround the Union trenches to enfilade them, but were forced to retire, when they had got within 150 feet of their objective, leaving twenty-five killed and wounded behind them. The Union force lost eleven men, of whom three were officers, and forty wounded.

Meanwhile, the southern army was actively engaged. Sir Duncan Mackenzie's column had dispersed the Germans and taken some booty from one or two places near Lüderitz Bay, and had seized many miles of railway. On February 22, 1915, his advance guard occupied Garub, a station seventy miles inland. Here a company of Union scouts pushed after the retiring Germans, and in a skirmish with mounted men protecting a troop train their leader was wounded. They were forced to retire, leaving one of their comrades a prisoner in the hands of the enemy. The British camp at Garub was also attacked by a hostile aeroplane which dropped hand grenades and shells, but there were no casualties.

Aus, an important station fifteen miles from Garub, was next occupied by Mackenzie. The place was evacuated without a struggle, but it showed that much work had been done to fortify it, and that the enemy had intended to resist. Owing to the rapid movements of the British force the Germans had abandoned everything, though several mines exploded when the town was occupied.

Turning now to the movements of General Smut's army in the south. Colonel Van der Venter, who commanded an important section of the army, crossed the Orange River and occupied a group of stations, including Nabas, Velloor, Ukamas, Jerusalem, and Heirachabis.

On the last day of March, 1915, Van der Venter's force was engaged in several skirmishes in which one man was killed and two wounded, while six of the enemy were killed and twenty-eight taken prisoners. At this price, the stations of Platbeen and Geitsand which yielded a great quantity of supplies and horses and live-stock were occupied.

On April 30, 1915, Van der Venter occupied Warmbad, the railway terminus, without opposition and pushing forward along the line his men entered Kabus, a station sixty-five miles to the north, two days later.

General Smut met Van der Venter at Kalkfontein on April 11, 1915, where plans were laid to drive the Germans from Karas Mountains where they occupied some strong positions. The enemy was attacked in three columns, advancing from different points. Finding themselves threatened on all sides, the Germans made no resistance and abandoned everything.

On April 17, 1915, Van der Venter entered Seeheim, the Germans fleeing in such hot haste that they could not stop to destroy the bridge over the Great Fish River. Colonel Berrange's force which had set out from Kimberley was now in touch with Van dev Venter's column. At Hasnur near Rietfontein, Berrange took an entrenched position with slight losses and after frequent skirmishes and hard fighting joined Van der Venter's forces near Keetmanshoop, which surrendered to the combined forces April 20, 1915.

Sir Duncan Mackenzie's column left at Aus now struck out to the northeast with his mounted men and occupied the towns of Bethany and Berseba without meeting resistance and April 24, 1915, reached Aritetis on the railway, seventy miles north of Keetmanshoop, General Mackenzie could now act in conjunction with Van der Venter against the Germans retreating from Seeheim and Keetmanshoop. At Kabus, twenty miles north, in an indecisive engagement with the enemy, the Union forces lost twenty-two men taken prisoners, while the Germans numbering about 600, continued their retreat, their objective being Gibeon, where they hoped to entrain for the capital, Windhoek. General Mackenzie therefore sent a small party to destroy the railway to the north of Gibeon, while the Ninth Brigade was to engage the enemy. This body was defeated by the Germans with severe loss. They took some seventy prisoners and forced the Ninth Brigade to fall back on the main body.

On the morning of April 28, 1915, Mackenzie led his whole force against the Germans in a dashing attack that drove them from the field, and his cavalry continued to pursue them over twenty miles of country. The rocky and irregular character of the ground in this neighbourhood made it difficult for cavalry operations, and the Germans made good their escape. The British lost three officers and twenty men killed; the wounded numbered fifty-five, of whom eight were officers. Among the killed was Major J. H. Watt of the Natal Light Horse. The British captured from the enemy seven officers, and about 200 men. They also released seventy of their own soldiers who had been made prisoners by the Germans on the previous day.

The booty that fell to the victors included field guns and Maxims, transport wagons, and large numbers of livestock. It was at Gibeon, where this battle was fought, that Sir George Farrar was killed in a railroad accident on May 18, 1915. His important services in the Commissariat Department during the invasion of the colony had contributed to making the successes of the Union forces possible. His career had been full of adventure. He was sentenced to death for the part he had taken in the Jamieson raid, and had fought against the Boers in 1899-02.

While General Mackenzie was successfully operating around Gibeon, General Botha's troops were active in the north; but nothing of importance occurred until May 1, 1915, when Kubas was hurriedly evacuated by the Germans and occupied by General Brits. Here, it was discovered that the Germans had made elaborate preparations for resistance, but—became panic-stricken by the sudden and unexpected arrival of Union forces. Miles of intrenchments surrounded the place, and a hundred contact mines were discovered and removed. From this point Colonel Brits continued his advance, and encountered the enemy at Otyimbigue, sixty-one miles from the capital of Windhoek. After a spirited skirmish the place was taken, the Germans losing twenty-eight men as prisoners. Continuing his victorious advance, the Union forces captured Karibib, an important railroad junction, and Johann Albrechtshöhe and Wilhelmstal were next occupied.

With General Botha threatening the capital from the west, and all the colony south of Gibeon in British hands, the greatest difficulties in the way of the invaders had been successfully overcome, and the end seemed to be near.

On May 10, 1915, General Botha was informed that Windhoek, the capital, was prepared to surrender. He set out at once for the town in a motor car accompanied by a small escort, and arranged with the Burgomaster of Windhoek the terms of capitulation.

On May 12, 1915, General Myburgh and a detachment of Union forces entered the town which contained at the time about 3,000 Europeans and some 12,000 natives.

Before the courthouse, in the presence of the town officials, and Union officers and men, a proclamation by General Botha in Dutch, English, and German was read, which placed the conquered districts under martial law, and which further expressed the hope that there would be no attempts to resist the Union forces as they must prove futile. The great wireless station at the capital, which kept the colony in touch with Berlin, was found to be uninjured, and with its capture the Germans lost their last wireless station outside of Europe. Thousands of cases of ammunition and parts of guns were among the prizes taken, while on the railway a number of locomotives and quantities of rolling stock were seized.

It now became the immediate business of General Botha's army to deal with those German straggling forces which remained still under arms in the north. In a few days following the occupation of the capital. Colonel Mentz found part of the enemy at Seeis, and without losing a man took 252 prisoners and a great quantity of booty. General Botha meanwhile occupied Omaruru, a station on the railway, and in the same week took possession of Kalkfield which was strongly entrenched, but which the Germans were compelled to abandon owing to Botha's adroit flanking movements. The Germans declining to make a stand, Botha's army swept victoriously onward.

In the last week in June, 1915, all the districts around Waterberg were cleared of the enemy. Leaving Okaputu in the evening of June 80, 1915, General Manie Botha with the Fifth Brigade got in touch with the Germans at dawn the next day near Osib, after a forced march of forty-two miles in sixteen hours. The Germans were driven off, and before nightfall Otavi was occupied. Here a good supply of water was found and as the country around is arid and like a desert, the loss of the town was a serious one to the enemy.

General Lukin with another brigade had set out from Omarasa at the same time as Manie Botha, and between them came General Botha and the Headquarters Staff.

The fight at Otavi was the last stand of importance made by, the

Germans. They had shown great bravery, but supplies were failing, they had been driven into the most inhospitable part of the colony, the natives were not always frigidly, and during the first days of July, 1915, they made preparations to surrender.

The Union troops under General Myburgh, having left the railway, encountered a body of Germans sixteen miles south of Tsumeb and in the skirmish, that followed, lost one man and took eighty-six prisoners.

At Tsumeb, which Myburgh entered on July 8, 1915, some 600 more prisoners were taken, while he was able to release a number of Union comrades who had been left behind by the Germans in their hurried retreat. Colonel Brits had by this time reached the German port of Namutoni, where he took 150 prisoners, and released some Union captives, the last that remained in German hands.

Dr. Seitz, the Governor of German South West Africa, now opened communications with General Botha concerning a surrender, and received the Union officer's terms in the form of an ultimatum. Botha stated that he and his troops stood ready to fight, if need be, another battle, but his terms were accepted before the time limit he had fixed expired.

At two o'clock in the morning of July 9, 1915, at a spot called Kilometre 500, General Botha, Dr. Seitz the Governor, and Colonel Francke, commander of the German troops in South West Africa, signed the terms of capitulation. All the Germans surrendered unconditionally. Officers were released on parole, and were free to live where they pleased in the country. The regular troops were permitted to retain their rifles, but no ammunition, and were interned for the remainder of the war in charge of one of their officers. The *Landwehr* and *Landsturm* of the reserve forces were permitted to retain their horses, but no arms, and were released on parole, and could return to their homes.

The formal surrender of the prisoners was held at Otavi, July 11, 1915, where General Lukin who was in charge of the details took over 204 officers, and 3,293 of other ranks; thirty-seven field guns and twenty-two machine guns. By the conquest of German South West Africa 322,450 square miles of territory, 113,670 more miles than all Germany, came under the British flag.

The suppression of the rebellion at home, and the invasion and conquest of this large territory had been accomplished by the Union forces with comparatively small loss of life considering the great num-

PORT
ALEXANDER

GREAT
FISH BAY

GUINEA (PORTUGUESE)

HANDA

HUMBE

CUNENE R.

O OMONDONGA

OKARANGO R.

MAI-INIS

C
FRIO

OKONDJU

GERMAN

O OTJITUO

MOREMI

O KOBIS

OTYZONDYOPAT

BHURAMBA R.

O GHANZE

SOUTHWEST

O KARIBIB

O SEEIS

O OTJINBIADE

O TWASS

CAPE CROSS

O WINDHOEK

O GOBABIS

SWAKOPMUND

SWAKOP R.

AFRICA

NOSOB R.

OVB R.

WALFISH BAY
(BRITISH)

O SCHEPPMANSDORF

SANDWICH
HARBOR

O KALKFONT

O KOWES

HOLLAMS BIRD I.
(BR.)

URIKOS

O GIBEON

O KOES

MOLOPO R.

BEERSHEBA

O KEETMANSHOOP

ANGRA PEQUENA
(LUDERITZ BAY)

BETHANY

SEEHEIM

KARAS
MTS.

O KALKFONTAIN

O GOBASTI

POSSESSION I.
(BRITISH)

KANIBES

NABABAS

ANGRA JUNTAS B.

WARMBAD

ORANGE R.

ORANGE R.

PORT NOLLOTH

WALFISH BAY
CAPE TOWN
800 MILES

O RONDABLE

O CARNARVON

OLIFANT R.

O CALVINIA

FRASERBURG

SOUTH ATLANTIC OCEAN

BRITISH SOUTH AFRICA

**HEAVY BLACK LINE
SHOWS ADVANCE OF
UNION TROOPS**
⊢⊢⊢ RAILROADS
SCALE OF MILES
0   50   100   200

ber of engagements that were fought in a most difficult country for military operations. The best estimate gives 1,612 for both campaigns. The killed numbered 406, of whom ninety-six were killed in action by the Germans and ninety-eight by the rebels, fifty-eight died of wounds, and 153 by disease, accident, and other causes, and 606 were taken prisoners. The losses to the rebels were 190 killed and between 300 and 350 wounded. The Germans lost 103 killed, and 195 wounded. Before the surrender the Union forces held 890 German prisoners in South West Africa.

While it is true that the Union troops greatly outnumbered the Germans, General Botha's conquest of the colony was none the less a brilliant military achievement The most dangerous foe that the Union soldiers encountered was not the Germans, but the deadly climate ; the stretches of burning desert *veld* from eighty to a hundred miles wide, that had to be crossed in a heat that rose at times to 120° Fahrenheit in the shadow of the tents. All the supplies, the provisions for the men, and much of the water for their consumption had to be brought from Cape Town. The care taken in the commissariat department, and especially in the water supply, in a country where the enemy had polluted the wells, accounted for the general good health of the invading army. That 30,000 men should have been able to fight in such a difficult country for five months at a cost of less than 2,000 casualties was an experience rare in military annals, and reflects lasting credit on General Botha who planned the entire invasion.

The Germans, outmatched and outnumbered, avoided engagements whenever possible, but offered a stubborn resistance and fought with great bravery when there was no alternative. Once the Union forces were ready to advance, their rapid movements and forced marches took the Germans by surprise in the midst of their preparations, and baffled and bewildered them. Cut off entirely from help from the outside, and running short of ammunition which could not be replaced, their struggle could only result in one conclusion.

www.ingramcontent.com/pod-product-compliance
Lightning Source LLC
Chambersburg PA
CBHW031854090426
42741CB00005B/489